#Draining the Swamp

How Trump's America First Agenda will Stop the Unraveling of America & Guarantee him a Second Term in the White House!

Patriotic Medic

#DRAINING *the* SWAMP

How Trump's America First Agenda will Stop the Unraveling of America & Guarantee him a Second Term in the White House!

Printed in the USA by Inspired Learning Group LLC

Published by Patriotic Medic, Scottsdale, AZ 85252

Edited by a "Patriotic friend" of Patriotic Medic

Email: Patrioticmedic@gmail.com or visit: patrioticmedic.com

Table of Contents

1

AN UNLIKELY CANDIDATE ENTERS THE RACE

IT WAS LIKE THE "SHOT" that was heard around the world! Donald J. Trump was going to enter the race for the White House. According to Wikipedia, "Trump formally announced his candidacy for the upcoming race for president in the 2016 election on June 16, 2015. He held a campaign rally at Trump Tower in New York City; in his speech, Trump drew attention to domestic issues such as illegal immigration, offshoring of American jobs, the U.S. national debt, and Islamic terrorism, in a campaign strongly emphasized by the slogan, "Make America Great Again." Trump declared that he would self-fund his presidential campaign, and would refuse any money from donors and lobbyists."

Following the announcement, most of the media's attention focused on Trump's comment on illegal immigration where he stated: *"When Mexico sends its people, they're not sending their best... They're sending people that have lots of problems, and they're bringing those problems with [them]. They're bringing drugs.*

They're bringing crime. They're rapists. And some, I assume, are good people." Trump's statement was controversial and led several businesses and organizations—including NBC, Macy's, Univision, and NASCAR—to cut ties with Trump in the following days. Reactions from other presidential candidates were mixed: some Republican candidates disagreed with the tone of Trump's remarks yet supported the core idea that illegal immigration is an important campaign issue, while other Republican candidates, along with the leading Democratic candidates, condemned Trump's remarks and his policy stances as offensive or inflammatory.[1]

COMING DOWN THE ESCALATOR!

I watched the entirety of Donald Trump's announcement via the popular social media site "YouTube." After he finished his speech, I knew that a different kind of political candidate had just entered the presidential race. Even though he was a famous TV icon, he was nevertheless a complete political outsider. He was also politically incorrect in every sense of the word. Notwithstanding, his lack of political correctness was quite refreshing to an American electorate that was tired of being forced into silent submission to winds of political correctness that were hell bent on stripping them of their constitutionally protected right to free speech. I knew instantly Donald Trump's candidacy would shake things up in American politics. Whether he would last a couple weeks or gain traction in the heavily contested republican presidential primaries was uncertain. Political pundits and the mainstream media quickly dismissed his candidacy as a publicity stunt by an egomaniac desperate for attention! Many thought he was doing it to boost the ratings of his highly successful show, *The Apprentice.*

Calls for Donald Trump to drop his presidential bid or apologize for suggesting that the Mexican government was sending some of its rapists and drug dealers to the United States through our porous southern border went unanswered. Instead of cowering and retreating in fear, as is the case with most Washington politicians, "the Donald" just doubled down. He refused to apologize, while the mainstream media begged him to do so, as though they cared about the posterity of his presidential campaign. He stood his ground, even when multinational corporations were canceling business contracts with him at great financial cost to himself. Never mind that he was already bleeding money by choosing to self-fund his presidential bid instead of running to the donor class with an offering plate in hand. Macy's was one of the major retailers that dropped their business association with him and Trump did not mince his words when he told attendees at his rallies what he thought of the CEO of Macy's. Thousands of Trump supporters cancelled their Macy's membership and cut up their Macy's credit cards.

I watched all of this with great amusement and admiration. I had never seen such political pressure from both political parties and the mostly biased mainstream media directed at one man! I kept asking myself, "Is Donald Trump going to collapse emotionally or capitulate to the political correctness of his fellow Republican presidential candidates and the mainstream media? How was his family dealing with the backlash caused by his presidential bid? What about the polls? Were they going to confirm what the political pundits predicted: *a failed, and dead on arrival presidential bid?*

On Fox News Sunday with Chris Wallace, political pundits such as George Will, Charles Krauthammer and Juan Williams predicted that Donald Trump would never become the President of the United States, let alone win the nomination for the Republican Party. In George Will's case his visceral hatred for Donald Trump was visible and disconcerting. CNN anchors such as Anderson Cooper and Don Lemon, and HBO's Bill Maher couldn't hide their disdain for what they felt was a buffoonery candidate who had no chance of winning the White House.

Bill Maher asked conservative writer and New York Times bestselling author of "Adios America," Ann Coulter, who she thought had the best chance of winning the Republican presidential nomination. When she mentioned Donald Trump's name, Bill Maher, his guests on the show, and the entire TV audience burst out in uncontrollable fits of laughter. Jerry Seinfeld couldn't have cracked a better joke had he been entertaining the audience. The heartfelt laughter of Bill Maher's TV audience, told a story...Donald Trump could never become President of the United States...and anybody who even suggested such a possibility however slim, was flirting with insanity. As far as they were concerned the verdict was in: *Donald Trump had zero chance of winning the presidency!*

Republican voters would have to be fools to vote for such a despicable man, surely, they would wake up just in time to nominate safer candidates like John Kasich or call Mitt Romney out of retirement for another shot at the goal. Encouraged by the rising numbers of "#NeverTrumpers" within the Republican Party, the pundits and political prognosticators patted each other on the back as they waited for their analysis to be proven true.

POLLS, POLLS, POLLS!

When the polls started coming in many pundits were both speechless and baffled. Donald Trump was up in the polls. In a few weeks he was number one in most opinion polls and stayed that way until he clinched the highly coveted Republican presidential nomination after eliminating 17 highly qualified candidates. In the process, Donald Trump garnered the largest number of primary voters (over 13 million) that have ever voted for a presidential candidate in the history of the Republican Party. I have since followed Donald Trump's presidential bid almost religiously because he is the most unpredictable and unscripted politician I have ever seen in my lifetime. I was fascinated by how his off-the-cuff comments made politics interesting again. Comments that would have doomed most political candidates only caused him to rise in the polls. His speeches to the American people in his rallies were not the doctored and overanalyzed teleprompter speeches we have come to expect from traditional politicians. I am convinced that the presidential bid of Donald Trump will go down in American history as the most consequential presidential bid in U.S. history!

Without a doubt Donald Trump's landslide victory over the most favored woman presidential candidate in U.S. history, Hillary Rodham Clinton, has sent shock waves in the polling industry. I predict that many polling companies that we have known for years are going to be closing shop or redirect their business model from predicting political elections to polling consumer-shopping habits. How could they have been so wrong in their prediction models concerning the candidacy of Donald Trump? Days before the election, polling companies were giving Hillary Clinton an 85% chance of winning the presidential election. For most of us who were silent Trump supporters, the morning of November 8th had a chilling effect. My wife and I registered for early voting and voted for the Trump-Pence ticket before we flew to Africa.

When the night of November 8th came I was glued to the television in the Republic of Zambia. I was staying as a guest at the house of the former Deputy Minister of Finance for the Republic of Zambia. Since much of Africa does not televise the Fox News Channel, I was left with having to watch the coverage of election results on left leaning news outlets such as CNN and BBC. I also found myself having to educate many of my fellow African friends and family members who had been told by the liberal press that Trump was a hardcore racist, who hated black people, and other minorities.

Early on CNN's coverage of the election returns, it was clear that all the CNN anchors appeared very confident that it was going to be an early night of victory for their preferred candidate, Hillary Clinton. After all, all the respected pollsters had already predicted a landslide election for the first woman presidential candidate. Both anchors and contributors were quick to point to the polls as they salivated over what they were sure was going to be a very good night for Democrats. I sat there and listened and started resigning myself emotionally to a Trump loss. As a concerned African American immigrant citizen who has feverishly followed the political life of the Clintons, since Clinton versus Bob Dole, I knew that the rapid decline of the United States, politically, economically, and socially would only accelerate under a Hillary Clinton presidency.

While I personally loved President Bill Clinton, everything his wife touched politically either fell apart or got corrupted. The ongoing Hillary Clinton email scandal at the State Department only strengthened my belief that while a Hillary win would have been historic, it would have simultaneously unleashed corruption in public office on a scale never before seen in American politics.

MIRACLE: A TRUMP LANDSLIDE

I listened to the political pundits who were predicting a Hillary win say that reliable sources within the Clinton campaign were very confident that Hillary Clinton was going to win the State of Florida. "If Trump loses the State of Florida, it's going to be an early night for the Hillary Campaign." One of the pundits on CNN declared. Trump needed to win Florida, North Carolina, Ohio, and Iowa in order for him to even have a prayer at winning the presidency. Any pro Trump commentators who appeared on CNN, MSNBC and BBC were very measured and borderline fearful in their predictions of a Trump win.

As I listened to the election night commentary, I became despondent because none of the pundits or news anchors of any of the major news networks spent any meaningful time on the possibility of a Hillary loss. How could she lose? Her victory was a foregone conclusion. She had a bulletproof "Blue Wall" (states that were historically solidly democratic, e.g., Michigan, Wisconsin, Pennsylvania) with a total of 53 Electoral College votes that would ensure a "W" for the first Democratic female presidential candidate, who had already spent over 1.2 billion-dollars hedging her chances.

What's more the exit polls were all pointing to a Hillary win and a devastating loss for the Trump-Pence ticket and for the Republican Party. Democrats were so confident in the election results that they even thought that they were going to get back control of the Senate, and possibly the House of Representatives. For a while the election returns in Florida were pointing to a Hillary win and you could sense the tension in the gloomy faces of Trump supporters at the Trump-Pence Election Headquarters in New York City.

While I was watching Donald Trump begin to catch up to Hillary in the vote count in Florida, the cable went off. I went to bed, depressed and resigned to a Trump loss. When I woke up early in the morning, the cable was back on. Imagine my surprise and bewilderment when I discovered that "the Donald" had not only won Florida, he had won a clean sweep of the important swing states. The look of doom and gloom on the faces of CNN and BBC news anchors who had been gloating when the night began and daydreaming on live television about announcing the presidency of the first woman president in U.S. history told me everything I needed to know. *The polls were wrong!* The lying main-stream-media was wrong! The highly paid and decorated political pundits were wrong! Boy, were they wrong!

THE BLUE WALL COLLAPSES!

When almost tearful liberal news anchors on CNN, MSNBC, ABC and BBC began to announce the beginning of the collapse of the impregnable "Blue Wall" of reliably democratic blue states of Pennsylvania, Wisconsin and

Michigan you knew then that the unthinkable had just happened. Donald Trump was about to become the 45th President of the United States. The glass ceiling had not been shattered.

The networks did everything they could to delay calling the blue state of Pennsylvania for Donald Trump, until it became increasingly embarrassing, even for them. Even with 99% of the results in and Donald Trump ahead of Hillary by over 70,000 votes, the networks were hopelessly looking for a miracle. The Associated Press was the first news organization to break away from the foolishness of hoping for a last-minute Hillary Clinton comeback win. They went ahead and called the State of Pennsylvania for a candidate they had previously said would never win the presidency!

THE BREATHTAKING PROJECTION!

Soon after the announcement of the Associated Press, other news organizations reluctantly began to make their own projections. It was like a bunch of dominoes began to fall.

- *CNN can now project that Donald Trump has won the State of Pennsylvania!*
- *ABC can now project that Donald Trump has won the State of Pennsylvania!*
- *MSNBC can now project that Donald Trump has won the State of Pennsylvania!*
- *BBC can now project that Donald Trump has won the State of Pennsylvania!*
- *FOX NEWS can now project that Donald Trump has won the State of Pennsylvania!*
- *CNN can now project that Donald Trump has just been elected the 45th President*

of the United States!

- *ABC can now project that Donald Trump has just been elected the 45th President of the United States!*
- *MSNBC can now project that Donald Trump has just been elected the 45th President of the United States!*
- *BBC can now project that Donald Trump has just been elected the 45th President of the United States!*
- *FOX NEWS can now project that Donald Trump has just been elected the 45th President of the United States!*

According to *The Gateway Pundit*, FOX News host Megyn Kelly looked like she was going to cry when Trump took the lead in the national vote. Anyone who watches Fox News knows that there is bad-blood between Megyn Kelly and Donald Trump dating back to the first Republican presidential debate when Megyn threw herself in the ring of presidential contenders with her famous "gotcha" question directed at Mr. Trump.

"You've called women you don't like fat pigs, dogs, slobs and disgusting animals." Megyn asked. *"Only Rosie O'Donnell!"* Donald replied, while the crowd laughed and cheered. In typical Trump style "the Donald" fired back at Megyn Kelly on Twitter moments after the debate. So, it's quite understandable why Trump's unexpected landslide win, unnerved the likes of Megyn Kelly. But she was not the only anchor of a major news network that was left speechless by the Trump win.

CNN's Van Jones had the most impassioned reaction to Donald

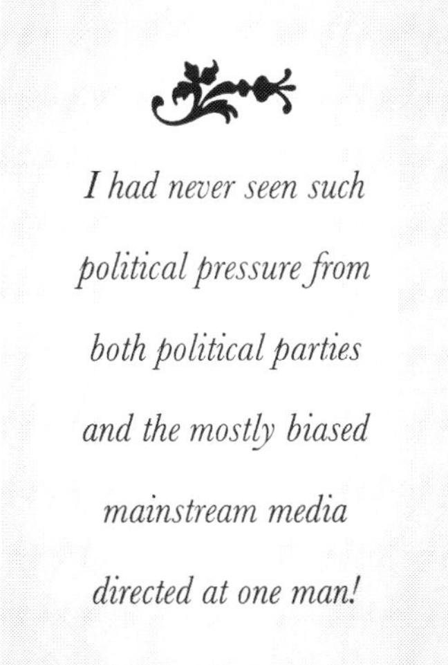

I had never seen such political pressure from both political parties and the mostly biased mainstream media directed at one man!

Trump's unexpected win. I watched an almost tearful and frustrated Van Jones try to make sense of what had just happened. He couldn't believe that the American people had actually voted into the White House a man the likes of him accused of bigotry, racism, xenophobia and every other sin known to man. In his opinion, he thought the election of Donald Trump was an affront to the first black president, comments Van Jones tried to walk back later. A look of shock, gloom and despair was clearly visible on the faces of the other news anchors and guest commentators on CNN.

Where was I, you might ask? I was on my feet dancing with joy, tears rolling down my face. I knew that ordinary "Joe" Americans, Caucasians, Hispanics, Asians and African-Americans had managed to see through the web of lies created by the corrupt mainstream media and political establishment to place a complete "outsider" into the Oval Office. I was not dancing because I believed even for a second that Donald Trump was the perfect candidate. It was clear to most of us Trump supporters that the "Donald" was a flawed candidate but he was not corrupt and his sincerity to "Make America Great Again" (#MAGA) was quite believable. The fact that he self-funded his own presidential campaign to stay clear of becoming the "Manchurian Candidate" controlled by powerful Washington lobbyists was quite refreshing to millions of us.

THE GREAT TRANSITION

Undoubtedly if the history of American presidential politics tells us anything, it is that there is a great transition between campaigning and governing. Very few presidential candidates who win the White House manage to deliver effectively on many of their campaign promises. Most especially, if they win the presidency but have to govern through a divided Congress. The cesspool of political corruption in Washington, D.C. manages to neutralize the political ambitions of most U.S. presidents.

Thankfully, Donald Trump voters across the fifty states knew this and delivered both the Senate and the House of Representatives. For an outsider who managed to anger many power brokers in both political establishments, governing with a divided Congress would have been next to impossible. The 45th President of the United States, Donald Trump, has to take advantage of time afforded to him to enact lasting changes, during what might be the shortest presidential honeymoon period in U.S. history. The first 100 days of his presidency are critical to making America great again!

THE FIRST 100 DAYS!

President Trump's first 100 days in office are as critical as any we have ever seen under any incoming president. The corrupt and biased mainstream news media, unhinged liberals, what's left of the Clinton machine, fake news propagandists, #Never-Trumpers die-hards, Washington lobbyists, not to mention a jilted political establishment, are going to go full throttle to oppose the success of a Trump presidency. Famed liberal filmmaker Michael Moore is already soliciting for fresh ideas on Twitter from his foot soldiers on how best to delegitimize a Trump presidency after his efforts to have Electoral College electors defect from voting for Trump on December 19, 2016 failed miserably.

With social wars on all fronts propagated by leftist militants, President Trump's agenda must be in full deployment in the first 100 days of his presidency. He needs to show his detractors and supporters that he meant business with the American people during his presidential campaign. During his highly attended political rallies, Candidate Trump unfolded his agenda for "Making America Great Again!"

I have taken the liberty to go through each agenda item in this book to remind us of what he promised to do. Most importantly it's an agenda that will only succeed if all Trump voters and ordinary Americans remain vigilant and engaged in the political process to cause beltway politicians in both political parties to remember the will of the American people. The American people, especially in the blue states of Wisconsin, Michigan and Pennsylvania voted to elect Donald Trump, precisely because of what he promised to do during his Presidential campaign. Trump's agenda, if implemented, will stop the unraveling of America and re-ignite the U.S economy for the better. If the Trump agenda is implemented:

- ✓ America will become great again!
- ✓ America will become safe again!
- ✓ America will become rich again!
- ✓ America will become respected again on the world stage!

2

DRAIN THE SWAMP

On October 18, 2016, then presidential candidate Donald Trump posted the following article on his campaign website (donaldjtrump.com). I will quote it verbatim and then expound on how the implementation of this aspect of the Trump agenda can radically transform politics in Washington, D.C. and give the government of the people back to the people. In laying this agenda here, I am in no way suggesting that President Trump will be successful at implementing this aspect of his agenda. But if he succeeds at even accomplishing 50% of the drain the swamp strategy the United States of America will be better for it. 50% less corrupt lobbyist money flowing in Washington can only slow this country's rapid decline towards financial and social destruction. Too much corrupt money from the Washington donor class has taken

Too much corrupt money from the Washington donor class has taken the government of the people by the people from the people

the government of the people by the people from the people. This is why Americans on both sides of the political divide no longer feel like Washington beltway politicians speak for them.

THE ANNOUNCEMENT

"There is another major announcement I am going to make today as part of our pledge to drain the swamp in Washington. If I am elected president, I will push for a constitutional amendment to impose term limits on all members of Congress. Decades of failure in Washington, and decades of special interest dealing, must come to an end. We have to break the cycle of corruption, and we have to give new voices a chance to go into government service. The time for Congressional term limits has arrived.

If we let the Clinton Cartel run this government, history will record that 2017 was the year America lost its independence. We will not let that happen. It is time to drain the swamp in Washington, D.C.

That is why I am proposing a package of ethics reforms to make our government honest once again.

First: I am going to institute a 5-year ban on all executive branch officials lobbying the government after they leave government service.

Second: I am going to ask Congress to institute its own 5-year ban on lobbying by former members of Congress and their staffs.

Third: I am going to expand the definition of lobbyist so we close all the loopholes that former government officials use by labeling themselves consultants and advisors when we all know they are lobbyists.

Fourth: I am going to issue a lifetime ban against senior executive branch officials lobbying on behalf of a foreign government.

Fifth: I am going to ask Congress to pass a campaign finance reform that prevents registered foreign lobbyists from raising money in American elections."[1]

CONGRESSIONAL TERM LIMITS: WHAT A NOBLE IDEA?

"If I am elected president, I will push for a constitutional amendment to impose term limits on all members of Congress. Decades of failure in Washington, and decades of special interest dealing, must come to an end. We have to break the cycle of corruption, and we have to give new voices a chance to go into government service. The time for Congressional term limits has arrived." Donald Trump, 10.18.16

Trump's drain the swamp strategy starts out with a bold but noble idea; *imposing term limits on members of Congress*. Candidate Trump promised to push for a constitutional amendment to impose terms limits on members of Congress. This aspect of the Trump agenda is one that will definitely find tremendous grassroots support from voters of both major political parties, including those who never voted for Trump. Ordinary everyday Americans and even those who are politically active know that Washington is fundamentally broken. This is why Congress consistently polls very low when ordinary Americans are asked how they feel about the work Congress is doing.

Unfortunately power brokers and lobbyists in both political establishments are going to fight very aggressively against such a sweeping Constitutional amendment. This is because both Republicans and Democrats don't want Congressional term limits because once you taste and grow fat on the Washington political gravy train you never want to get off the train, even if staying on the train dooms the whole country. How else do you explain these stupid one-sided trade deals that politicians of both parties have been voting for, for years? Today's Washington, D.C. politicians are a far cry from the founding fathers who did not see public service as a permanent career path. Many of them were hardcore patriots who entered politics for the public good and many of them quickly returned to their day job after the end of their public service.

Imposing a constitutional amendment mandating terms limits on members of Congress would be the quickest way to drain the swamp of corruption in our nation's capital. Term limits would cause members of Congress to be more aware of their fiduciary responsibility towards the people who elected them, e.g., their constituents. Congressional term limits would also reduce the appeal that today's politics has as the quickest get-rich-scheme in town. Public servants are not supposed to get rich off their public service. A political system such as this is both toxic and burdensome on maintaining the integrity of a constitutional republic, like the United States of America. When politics becomes big business public service takes a back seat and voters become victims of a political system that does not represent them or their interests.

However, imposing a constitutional amendment mandating terms limits on members of Congress is easier said than done, because article 5 (V) of the United States Constitution requires the consent of a three-fourth majority of Congress or the States in order to make any amendments to the Constitution. Can you imagine President Trump marshaling a three-fourth majority of Congressional republicans and democrats in both houses for an amendment that will in effect limit their political power and give it back to the people?

I am hopeful but I don't think Trump supporters should put too much stock in this aspect of the drain swamp strategy. But if President Trump fails to compel Washington beltway politicians or the States from going along with his very noble proposal to impose term limits on members of Congress, it won't be for lack of effort on his part. Telling politicians to curtail their power is like telling a prostitute to stop selling her body when business is booming. Below is the exact wording of article V of the Constitution for those of you who may not know what it says.

"The Congress, whenever two thirds of both Houses shall deem it necessary, shall propose Amendments to this Constitution, or, on the Application of the Legislatures of two thirds of the several States, shall call a Convention for proposing Amendments, which, in either Case, shall be valid to all Intents and Purposes, as part of this Constitution, when ratified by the Legislatures of three fourths of the several States, or by Conventions in three fourths thereof, as the one or the other Mode of Ratification may be proposed by the Congress; Provided that no Amendment which may be made prior to the Year One thousand eight hundred and eight shall in any Manner affect the first and fourth Clauses in the Ninth

Section of the first Article; and that no State, without its Consent, shall be deprived of its equal Suffrage in the Senate."

ANALYZING THE FIVE PILLARS OF THE DRAIN THE SWAMP STRATEGY

We will now analyze what I call the five pillars of Trump's drain the swamp strategy.

First: I am going to institute a 5-year ban on all executive branch officials lobbying the government after they leave government service.

This is breathtaking to say the least. Can you imagine how this proposal, once enacted into law, would drain the swamp of corruption in Washington, D.C.? A five-year ban on all executive branch officials lobbying the government after they leave service would make influence peddling by former government officials much less appealing. The fear of going to jail for violating this five-year ban would make former government officials much more difficult to seduce by Washington lobbying firms in search of either lucrative government contracts or favorable legislation. President Trump's pledge to institute a 5-year ban can't come soon enough.

If things in Washington, D.C. stay as they are the cesspool of corruption will only get worse and the people who will be left holding the tab are hardworking everyday Americans. Currently, a lobbying firm can hire executive branch officials immediately after they leave government service.

You don't have to be a rocket scientist to figure out why lobbying firms go into a bidding war to lure the service of a former executive branch official who still has deep ties to the White House.

Both Democrats and Republicans take advantage of this loophole in the lobbying laws of the United States, but politicians from either party would have a very difficult time explaining their opposition to a bill meant to restrict corruption and the power the lobbying industry has over ex-government officials. Unlike the constitutional amendment imposing congressional term limits that requires a three-fourth majority for passage, this Trump proposal to drain the swamp by imposing a five-year ban on lobbying by former executive branch officials would easily find footing for bipartisan support.

Second: I am going to ask Congress to institute its own 5-year ban on lobbying by former members of Congress and their staffs.

This second aspect of President Trump's drain the swamp strategy is just as refreshing as the first. When members of Congress are running for Senate or the House of Representatives they do so by promising the American people that they will go to Washington to clean up Washington. Every election cycle U.S. voters are exposed to impassioned speeches by candidates running for office, promising them a government that works for average citizens and represents their interests. While there is always a faithful few who deliver on their campaign promises, most political freshmen get swallowed by a political machinery controlled by lobbyists and elites. Most are bribed into submissive silence by being given their own portion of the Washington gravy train. Once their silence has been bought and paid for, complicity follows. I want to quote verbatim an article written by the website (represent.us) on how the lobbying industry corrupts or buys off members of Congress.

Lobbyists routinely offer members of Congress and their staffers lucrative jobs at their firms or their clients' companies. These negotiations often take place while our representatives are still in office and, ostensibly, working for us, the American people. With multi-million-dollar future salaries on the line, most members of Congress are more than willing to protect the best interests of the lobbyists who will one day be their employers.

"I would say to [the Member], 'When you're done working on the Hill, we'd very much like you to consider coming to work for us.' **The moment I said that, we owned them.** And what does that mean? Every request from our office, every request of our clients, everything that we want, they're gonna do." – Former lobbyist Jack Abramoff

> *The phenomenon of members of Congress heading off to work for lobby-ing firms and their clients is know as* ***"the revolving door."*** *And it's become shockingly common: in the 1970s, less than 5% of retiring legislators went on to become lobbyists. Now, half of retiring senators and a third of retiring house members do."*[2]

Without a doubt the above article illustrates why President Trump's second proposal on how to drain the swamp of corruption in Washington, D.C. is a much needed and long awaited remedy to correcting what's wrong with American politics. We do not stand in long election lines waiting to cast our vote to send politicians to Washington so they can have coveted political positions on select committees that they can leverage to advance their own selfish interests.

How many of us, Republican, Democrat or Independent would have voted for the people we voted for if we had a crystal ball that showed us that they would simply become lap-dogs for the Washington donor class, instead of fighting for the American people? This is why I believe that these aspects of President Trump's drain the swamp strategy are going to be met with bipartisan support because of political pressure from the grass roots. Americans of all races and walks of life are tired of a broken Washington, D.C. that only works for political elites, multinational corporations and the donor class.

Third: I am going to expand the definition of lobbyist so we close all the loopholes that former government officials use by labeling themselves consultants and advisors when we all know they are lobbyists.

The third aspect, of the five pillars of President Trump's drain the swamp strategy showcases why his candidacy scared establishment politicians in Washington, D.C. on both sides of the political divide. If you remember when candidate Trump was vying for the Republican presidential nomination during the primaries, he kept saying that he was self-funding his campaign because he knew the system having been on the other side of it as a member of the donor class. This is why he did not want to be beholden to the political pressure of lobbyists and the elite donor class, who are the invisible puppet masters of many of our notable politicians.

Only a person such as Donald Trump who has been part of the donor class, pulling the strings of bought-and-paid-for politicians, can say, "*I am going to expand the definition of lobbyist so we close all the loopholes that former government officials use by labeling themselves consultants and advisors when we all know they are lobbyists.*" Don't you think that the "Donald" knows what he is talking about here? As a member of the donor class he probably ran into a lot of former government officials who were selling their connections in Washington to the highest bidder, while masquerading as business consultants or advisors. But for someone like Trump who has wined and dined many of these former government officials, he knows how difficult it is for a leopard to hide it spots or a wolf its paws. This is why he is proposing expanding the definition of lobbyist to include former government officials who are lobbying the very institutions of government they led in the name of "consultants and advisors." Expanding the definition of the term lobbyist will definitely drain the swamp of corruption in Washington, D.C..

Fourth: I am going to issue a lifetime ban against senior executive branch officials lobbying on behalf of a foreign government.

The scandals involving the pay-to-play schemes surrounding the disgraced Clinton Foundation were exposed by investigative journalist and

New York Times bestselling author Peter Schweizer's book, Clinton Cash. According to an article written for the National Review by Myra Adams, a media and political writer, in which she states: "If anyone still doubts that the Clintons are greedy, corrupt, and morally reprehensible, they won't after this. The alleged fraud and corruption within the Clinton Foundation is, by now, old news to political junkies. It was all skillfully laid out last year in Peter Schweizer's bestselling book Clinton Cash.... The viewer is shown numerous examples of blatant pay-to-play schemes. These lucrative business deals illustrate the unofficial partnership between Clinton's State Department and the Clinton Foundation. Every scheme is perpetrated to personally enrich the Clintons, their Foundation, or their high-powered cronies — *in the name of "doing good" for the world's poor, naturally. Clinton Cash takes us on a whirlwind tour of Rwanda, the Congo, Nigeria, Haiti, Columbia, and India. We see how both Clintons impacted and influenced multi-million-dollar business deals involving Canada's Keystone XL pipeline and Ericsson, the international Sweden-based communications giant."* [3]

In light of the scandals involving the most blatant in-your-face pay-to-play schemes generated by both Clintons that was also criticized by some die-hard-Democrats, its not difficult to understand why President Trump made this fourth proposal on how to drain the swamp of corruption that has infected almost every branch of government, and politics in general. It's a very dangerous threshold to cross when we allow foreign money to begin to influence American foreign and domestic policy. Former executive branch government officials lobbying inside the United States on behalf of foreign oligarchs sets a very dangerous precedent, which in my opinion borders on treason. It's time to drain the swamp and "Make America Great Again!"

Fifth: I am going to ask Congress to pass a campaign finance reform that prevents registered foreign lobbyists from raising money in American elections."

I have a religious reaction to the fifth pillar of Trump's drain the swamp strategy, so I will simply say, "Amen!" In today's dangerous world were both nations and multinational corporations are being held hostage by terrorist organizations, high level espionage, political blackmail, and professional hackers, why would we ever want to have lobbying firms belonging to foreign countries putting money in our democratic elections?

Why would we want foreign influence in the elections of the land of the free and home of the brave? Whatever influence these organizations foster it will not be to the benefit of hardworking everyday Americans. I believe this is a campaign finance reform that should find both bipartisan support and that of American voters. If President Trump manages to implement his "drain the swamp strategy" he will be way on his way to "Making America Great Again!"

3

REPEAL AND REPLACE OBAMACARE

EVERY AMERICAN regardless of political ideology or none-thereof will agree that the Affordable Care Act commonly known, as Obamacare, is President Barak Obama's crowning achievement of his presidency. It's no wonder he and First Lady Michelle campaigned furiously for a presidential candidate (Hillary Clinton) that both of them could not stand. It's no secret that there was no love lost between the Clintons and the Obamas.

The blood feud between these two Democratic Party political dynasties is properly documented in Edward Klein's book, *Blood Feud*! The 2008 Democratic presidential primaries revealed deep cracks in the relationship between the Obamas and the Clintons. But political expedience heals all wounds political. In Obama's desire to preserve his legacy, having a candidate who could leave his signature achievement intact was enough to throw himself on the campaign trail to elect what would have been America's first female president.

On the other hand, the Republican presidential candidate Donald Trump did not mince his words letting people in his rallies now what he thought of Obamacare. On November 1, 2016 then candidate Trump released a speech he made on Obamacare on his campaign website and I quote.

" When we win on November 8th, and elect a Republican Congress, we will be able to immediately repeal and replace Obamacare. I will ask Congress to convene a special session.

Obamacare is a catastrophe. The President said if you like your plan you can keep your plan, if you like your doctor you can keep your doctor – which may go down as one of the great political lies of the century. Even the skeptical Democrats believed him and approved the legislation. No one even read the 2,700-page bill.

The Obama Administration has just announced massive double-digit and triple-digit Obamacare premium hikes everywhere in the country. Here, in Pennsylvania, premiums are going to increase more than 60 percent. That means parents won't have enough money to pay their bills, or get medicine for their kids. In the great state of Arizona, a wonderful place I just left, premiums will go up even higher than 116 percent – others states are going up more than 60, 70, 80, and 90 percent.

Deductibles can go to 12 thousand, 13 thousand, 14 thousand and even 15 thousand dollars. These deductibles are so high that your health care won't even be usable.

People all across the country are devastated. In many instances, thei. health care costs are more than their mortgage costs or rent, a first in American history. This is particularly unfair to millennials, and younger Americans generally, who will be totally crushed by these massive health care costs before they even get started on their journey through life.

One-third of the counties in Pennsylvania will have only a single insurance company. That includes Philadelphia.

The Associated Press found that "some of the 440,000 Pennsylvania consumers who buy insurance through healthcare.gov will face some of the highest premium increases in the nation."

Insurers are leaving, premiums are soaring, doctors are quitting, companies are fleeing, and deductibles are through the roof. Workers' hours are being cut, hiring is frozen, and wages are being slashed. Obamacare means higher prices, fewer choices, and lower quality.

> *Yet, Hillary Clinton wants to expand Obamacare and make it even more expensive. She wants to put the government totally in charge of health care in America. If we don't repeal and replace Obamacare, we will destroy American health care forever – it's one of the single most important reasons why we must win on November 8th."* [1]

The above Trump speech clearly demonstrates why President Barak Obama, the mainstream media and the liberal-left were heavily invested in seeing Hillary Clinton get elected to the White House. Her presidency would have assured the survival of President Obama's signature legislation. Hillary could have tinkered with ObamaCare for her own political survival but she would never have repealed it and most importantly she would have quickly transformed it into the holy grail of the liberal-left, e.g., a "single payer healthcare system."

What good is free if free kills you while you are waiting in line to see a doctor?

As an African American immigrant from Africa, I know first-hand that a single payer healthcare system, otherwise known as "socialized medicine" does not work. It always begins with good intentions by big government but quickly mushrooms into a nightmarish healthcare system, where patients wait in long lines for hours to see a doctor and in some cases a nurse. A single payer healthcare system also creates a dependent population of millions of citizens who are forced to compete for very few health care providers.

Something else liberals don't want to tell the American public when they are pushing the utopia of a healthcare system run and paid for by big government, the government that made all these grandeur promises quickly runs out of money to meet its financial obligations for the rising costs of an unsustainable healthcare system. What good is free if free kills you while you are waiting in line to see a doctor?

SAVED BY THE BELL!

On June 28th, 2012 ObamaCare (Patient Protection & Affordable Care Act) was saved by the bell in a 5-4 healthcare decision by the Supreme Court, with

Chief Justice Roberts siding with the liberal side of the Court. Unfortunately, this would not be the last time the pseudo-conservative Chief Justice a George Bush appointee, would manipulate the interpretation of the law to salvage the Affordable Care Act.

In saving ObamaCare in 2012, Chief Justice Roberts totally changed centuries of established interpretation of the Commerce Clause and whether this clause could be extended to, in effect, tax American citizens for essentially abstaining from participating in the healthcare law, as the ObamaCare mandate purported to do. In a scathing dissenting opinion, Justices Scalia, Thomas, Kennedy and Alito wrote:

Congress has set out to remedy the problem that the best health care is beyond the reach of many Americans who cannot afford it. It can assuredly do that, by exercising the powers accorded to it under the Constitution. The question in this case, however, is whether the complex structures and provisions of the Patient Protection and Affordable Care Act (Affordable Care Act or ACA) go beyond those powers. We conclude that they do.

> *This case is in one respect difficult: it presents two questions of first impression. The first of those is whether failure to engage in economic activity (the purchase of health insurance) is subject to regulation under the Commerce Clause. Failure to act does result in an effect on commerce, and hence might be said to come under this Court's "affecting commerce" criterion of Commerce Clause jurisprudence. But in none of its deci-*

> *sions has this Court extended the Clause that far. The second question is whether the congressional power to tax and spend, U. S. Const., Art. I, §8, cl. 1, permits the conditioning of a State's continued receipt of all funds under a massive state-administered federal welfare program upon its acceptance of an expansion to that program. Several of our opinions have suggested that the power to tax and spend cannot be used to coerce state administration of a federal program, but we have never found a law enacted under the spending power to be coercive. Those questions are difficult.* [2]

The decision by SCOTUS to save the "Affordable Care Act" as it did in 2012 was undoubtedly a short-term victory for President Barack Obama and Democrats who had rushed this massive healthcare bill (over 2000 pages long) into law on a partisan basis, without actually reading what was actually inside it. House Speaker Nancy Pelosi at the time ObamaCare was passed famously said, "We must pass it to see what is in it!" Unfortunately for her, over four years later most Americans have seen what is inside it and don't like it one bit. Outside of the shock caused by rising health insurance premiums, loss of their doctors caused by ObamaCare and the bleeding of American jobs to other countries because of bad trade deals, how can you explain an unconventional candidate like Donald Trump winning Blue Sates like Pennsylvania, Michigan and Wisconsin?

PASSED UNDER A CLOUD OF POLITICAL DECEPTION

I am a firm believer that "things don't end wrong, they start wrong!" This statement encapsulates my feelings about the passage and future of the so-called "Patient Protection & Affordable Care Act." ObamaCare was passed under a very partisan cloud of political deception. I don't even have to jolt my memory to remember some of the deceptions of the Affordable Care Act. I will quickly list the deceptions below that have already been proven to be the product of political trickery.

1. When President Obama was campaigning for the Patient Protection and Affordable Care Act he told the American public that they would never lose their doctor because of the healthcare law. Since its passage the healthcare law has completely contradicted the President's promise. Millions of Americans have since lost access to their primary doctor that many had gone to for years. Some doctors even quit practicing medicine to avoid the burdensome paperwork and bureaucratic red tape imposed upon them by ACA.

2. When President Obama was campaigning for the Patient Protection and Affordable Care Act he told the American public that the passage of the healthcare law would lead to a reduction in premiums of about $2000 per household. Once again this was not true. Many

Americans have seen their insurance premiums skyrocket by as much as 50-116%, in states like Arizona!

3. When President Obama was campaigning for the Patient Protection and Affordable Care Act he told the American public that the passage of the healthcare law would make healthcare affordable and protect them as patients. We have already seen that the "Affordable Care Act" is anything but affordable. Most importantly the law does little to protect patients but it does a lot to protect the insurance companies. But even the protections inside the law for insurance companies are falling through leading to major insurance companies like AETNA from getting out of the ObamaCare health exchanges.

4. When President Obama was campaigning for the Patient Protection and Affordable Care Act he told the American public that the passage of the healthcare law would not increase taxes on the middle class, except on the top 1 percent of income earners. In an article written for US News, by Nancy Pfotenhauer on July 23, 2012, she says the following about the Affordable Care Act.

"Now, the law was written purposefully to back-load the taxes—in other words, enjoy the upside now, pay the price later. It's like eating a large pizza with extra cheese and finding out two weeks from now that you don't fit into your jeans anymore. Only much, much worse: In

fact, according to the Joint Economic Committee, The "Cadillac tax" on high-cost health care isn't scheduled to take effect until 2018. But because the tax is linked to general inflation, and not medical inflation, it will hit more and more health plans over time – not just "Cadillac" insurance plans, but "Chevy" plans and even "Yugo" health plans.... The "high income" surtax is not indexed for inflation at all – it's designed to hit more and more middle-income families every year. Page 87 of the 2010 Medicare trustees report notes that the tax will hit only 3 percent of workers next year, when the tax takes effect – but a whopping 79 percent of all workers by 2080." [3]

SOME GOODIES IN OBAMACARE!

While the Patient Protection and Affordable Care Act is a seriously flawed law it has some goodies that conservatives and everyday Americans must not be too quick to throw down the toilet of repealing ObamaCare. This is why Trump's healthcare agenda is best discussed under the forensic lenses of "Repeal and Replace." Repealing the Affordable Care Act also upends its following provisions:

1. The ban on insurers denying coverage to individuals with pre-existing condition. I once worked as an insurance agent for a health insurance company and I can tell you by experience that it "sucks"

to have a pre-existing condition in the health insurance market. Most importantly, health insurance companies are very biased in their underwriting guidelines against people with pre-existing conditions. I came across people who used to be relatively healthy but when they used their health insurance once for a major surgery, the insurance companies found a way to drop them before a second health crisis and immediately they became almost uninsurable for any other health insurance company. I knew it was not fair but I was bound as an agent to toe the line.

2. Children living at home with their parents' can stay on their parents' health insurance plans for a period of time, until they are twenty-six years old. This is another goodie in the current version of the Affordable Care Act that I can appreciate as a former health insurance agent.

During his against-all-odds Presidential run, Donald Trump spoke about the importance of keeping these two popular provisions of the Affordable Care Act. Breaking from years of Republican tradition, he hinted at finding a government safety-net healthcare solution for the poorest Americans who can't afford healthcare. How this would look like in the "Replacement" part of his pledged "Repeal" of Obamacare is yet to be seen. In an interview with Lesley Stahl that aired on "60 Minutes," President-elect Trump said he would like to keep the portions of the Affordable Care Act requiring coverage of pre-existing conditions and children living at home under the age of twenty-six.

TRUMP'S HEALTH CARE PROPOSALS

As I stated earlier Donald Trump's healthcare agenda is best discussed under the forensic lenses of "Repeal and Replace." President-elect Trump's pick of representative Tom Price, as Secretary of Health and Human Services is a clear indication that he intends to go through with his campaign promise to repeal Obamacare. However, the appointment of Tom Price as Secretary of Health also means that Trump does not want to take too much time in replacing Obamacare. Tom Price, who has a medical background, is a known critic of the Affordable Care Act, but he has also been working on the best way to replace the flawed healthcare law for sometime. I believe this is why Trump chose him above the others he interviewed for this position.

Trump's healthcare proposal on the campaign trail was simple but profoundly practical. His proposals stem from the experiences he had over the years fighting with insurance companies while trying to buy the best healthcare insurance for thousands of employees of the Trump organization. Unfortunately, for the American public most of the politicians who voted for the Affordable Care Act, have never had to make payroll. They don't know how to create a job and what goes into securing good health insurance for one's employees. Trump has firsthand experience dealing with this issue. In a speech Trump made on November 1, 2016, which was later posted to his campaign site, he said:

"Our replacement plan includes Health Savings Accounts, a nationwide insurance market where you can purchase across state lines, and letting states manage Medicaid dollars. We will create quality, reliable, affordable health care in a free market where parents can make the health care decisions that are right for their families. It will be much better health care, at a much less expensive cost." November 1, 2016

FEATURES OF THE TRUMP PLAN

1. Allowing Americans to self-insure through Health Savings Accounts. In an article written by Peter Suderman on March 28, 2011 for the website reason.com, he makes an interesting case for Health Savings Accounts and I quote him in part.

"At Forbes, Dean Zarras makes a strong case for moving away from comprehensive health insurance and toward health savings accounts: In broad terms, Zarras is talking about moving toward consumer-driven health plans which couple HSAs with high-deductible health insurance. Experts are still studying the effects of those plans, but the evidence we have strongly suggests that they provide what traditional health insurance does not: lower overall cost, increased use of preventive care, and equal health outcomes. As I've noted before, a metastudy of high-quality research into consumer-drive plans conducted by the American Academy of Actuaries indicates that such plans result in big cost savings the first year after switching to a CDHP, and (though the evidence is less conclusive) smaller savings in years after that. That's a real achievement. The vast majority of the time you hear talk about

"reducing health costs," what you're really hearing about are proposals designed to reduce the projected growth in health spending. Consumer-driven plans seem to result in real savings—and without sacrificing quality of care." [4]

2. A nationwide insurance market where you can purchase insurance across state lines. One of the fallacies of our broken healthcare system that was designed for public consumption compliments of Washington, D.C. lobbying groups financed by insurance companies, is the fallacy of not allowing Americans or corporations to bid for health insurance across state lines. This is insane! Imagine if you cannot buy Coca Cola or gasoline by going across state lines? How foolish and unfair would this be? Yet our health insurance markets are so territorial, which only benefits the overstuffed insurance companies but hurts ordinary Americans in search of affordable healthcare. But here comes the "Donald" to the rescue! Force health insurance companies to compete against each other across state lines and watch the price of health care plummet without any tinkering from the Federal government.

3. Allowing states to manage Medicaid dollars. In an article written for the National Governors Association by Vernon K. Smith, Ph.D he makes the following observation.

"Medicaid is a State-Federal health care program created by the Social Security

Amendments of 1965. States administer the program within Federal guidelines. Over the years, Congress has added substantially to the scope of Medicaid, and as the program has expanded it has become increasingly important as a mechanism to finance health care for low-income children, families, pregnant women, the elderly and persons with disabilities. It also now finances a large share of mental health, public health and services for the aging. Over time Medicaid has become burdened with new requirements, and the costs for states have become greater than ever expected. Medicaid has grown to be larger than Medicare in terms of program costs and the number of persons served annually. The cost of Medicaid borne by states has become so large as to raise a question about the ability of states to pay their share in the future." [5]

In Dr. Vernon K. Smith's esteemed opinion Medicaid is being heavily burdened by ever-increasing demands placed upon it by the federal government. Making it difficult for states to effectively manage the ever-growing Medicaid program, plus afford the ever-growing costs of managing Medicaid on a state level. While most states have to be careful to balance their budgets, the federal government continues to spend and print money like a drunken sailor. This is why President Trump is suggesting having the states and not the federal government manage the Medicaid dollars allocated to them. He knows that when this becomes the case, states will spend those Medicaid dollars much more responsibly than some bureaucrat in Washington, D.C..

4. Place patients in charge of their health care decisions instead of bureaucrats in Washington, D.C.. Isn't this a noble idea? Who would have thought of this, ordinary Americans better at managing their healthcare decisions than some Washington bureaucrat? Certainly, this idea had to come from an outsider (Donald Trump) who has more faith in the wisdom of the American people than the all-knowing-power of the federal government. Anytime you place a bureaucrat between a patient and his doctor, you don't get better health care you always get more government.

5. Allow the power of the free market to determine the price of health insurance instead of selective and politicized tinkering by the Federal government. If America's history has taught us anything, its that the cornerstone of American exceptionalism is the free market. Each time the government gets out of the way of the free market" by removing burdensome regulations and allowing the "self-correcting" forces of free market such as competition, supply and demand to take over, wonderful things happen. Subjecting health insurance companies to the same across State lines forces of the free market that chain stores like Wal-Mart and Dillard's compete on, insurance costs will definitely go down.

FINAL ANALYSIS: MAIN REASON FOR OBAMACARE

In closing I want to ask a basic but fundamental question. "Why was Obamacare rushed into legislation, even when it was so flawed?" The flaws of Obamacare and its litter of broken promises are now self-evident. So why would the Democrats and President Obama hedge their political legacy on it? The real motive is political and has little to do with wanting millions of Americans to have access to affordable care. The latter was the "dangling carrot" that was used for the passage of the legislation, but the real motive was to place one-third of the American economy under the perennial control of the Democratic Party. It's the same utopian idea behind the Democratic Party's silent support for open borders and its reluctance to curb illegal immigration.

Having lived under a Socialist government led by Zambia's first President, Kenneth Kaunda, I know firsthand how "socialized medicine" gives the government almost god-like powers over its citizenry. It's also a very effective tool for moving the country into a one party state. Even in a two-party state like the United States, if the American public becomes addicted to free healthcare through Uncle Sam, they will also become addicted to voting for the political party that brought them this entitlement even when the costs of the program are driving the country into more national debt.

RULES FOR RADICALS

What most Americans, especially low information voters, don't know is that both President Barak Obama and Hillary Clinton are disciples of a socialist radical, Saul D. Alinsky, in both ideology and practice. Filmmaker Dinesh D'Souza does a great job of tabulating this in his two-bestselling documentaries, *Obama's America: Unmaking the American Dream* and *Hillary's America: the Secret History of the Democratic Party*. Saul D. Alinsky wrote a book that many Harvard liberals and some in the mainstream media revere as much as Christians revere the Bible, *Rules for Radicals*. This book has more to do with the real motives behind Obamacare than the desire to insure millions of Americans.

In Saul D. Alinsky's *Rules for Radicals*, there are eight levels of control that must be achieved before the creation of a socialist state. The first step is the most important of all. Can you guess what it is?

1. *Healthcare: Control healthcare and you control the people*
2. *Poverty: Increase the poverty level as high as possible, poor people are easier to control and will not fight back if you are providing everything for them to live.*
3. *Debt: Increase the debt to an unsustainable level. That way you are able to increase taxes, and this will produce more poverty.*
4. *Gun Control: Remove the ability to defend themselves from the government. That way you are able to create a police state.*
5. *Welfare: Take control of every aspect of their lives (food, housing, and income)*
6. *Education: Take control of what people read and listen to take control of what children learn in school.*
7. *Religion: Remove the belief in God from the government and schools*

8. *Class Warfare: Divide the people into the wealthy and the poor. This will cause more discontent and it will be easier to take (tax) the wealthy with the support of the poor.* [6]

Once you understand Saul D. Alinsky, Rules for Radicals, you quickly begin to understand that Obamacare or socialized medicine has little to do with the desire to give healthcare to millions of people as much as providing an avenue for increase of political control of the population. Socialized medicine is one of they key cornerstones of building a socialist state.

4

LOWER TAXES

"THERE is nothing more permanent than death and taxes." Fewer expressions capture the essence of the American experiment and spirit like the above statement. The genesis of the American Revolution can be traced back to the issues of taxes. Most Americans alive today cannot fully appreciate why the issue of taxes is so central to American democracy and our system of government. Have you ever heard of the Boston Tea Party?

At face value one would think this was an invitation to an actual tea party that was being held in Boston. Nothing could be further from the truth. The Boston Tea Party was the seed or impetus for the American Revolution of 1773. One of the campaign promises President-elect Trump made was to lower taxes across the board. Keeping this promise is essential to unleashing the forces of a new American renaissance. For Trump, lowering taxes across the board will be key to achieving one of his campaign war cries, *"We will make American rich again!"*

JESUS AND TAXES

While taxes are central to fueling the ongoing saga of the American Revolution and sustaining our federal and local governments, they were also a central issue in Jesus' day. Perhaps the seeds for the Boston Tea Party could be traced as far back as the oppressive, tax without representation policy of the Roman Empire. Most of America's founding fathers held a deep belief in the Bible and its teachings. The Bible shaped some of the framing of their understanding of taxation. Jesus was born in an environment where the Jewish people were reeling from the burden of undue taxation by their Roman governors. Once, his detractors asked him whether they should pay taxes to Caesar? His answer forever settled the issue of taxes.

God is not against the paying of taxes as fuel for propelling the engines of human government. *"Now tell us what you think about this: Is it right to pay taxes to Caesar or not?" But Jesus knew their evil motives. "You hypocrites!" he said. "Why are you trying to trap me? Here, show me the coin used for the tax." When they handed him a Roman coin, he asked, "Whose picture and title are stamped on it?" "Caesar's," they replied. "Well, then," he said, "give to Caesar what belongs to Caesar, and give to God what belongs to God (Mt 22:17-21)."*

As far as Jesus was concerned governments whose currency you use to trade in have the right to tax you. But taxes must be fair and not oppressively burdensome. When taxes are too high they become nothing more than legalized plunder by government. The progressive left always supports "legalized plunder by government" under the mantra "everyone has to pay their fair share of taxes," because in their view the number one enemy to the establishment of a socialist utopia is too much money in private hands. This is why they are so obsessed with finding ways to bankrupt what they call the top 1% of income earners. What they don't tell you is that on their way to plundering the money of the top 1% of income earners, they will take your money too. Don't worry; you will be just fine when all the money is in the hands of big government. Big government- will then pay for your healthcare, food, education and welfare. Destination: Socialism.

BOSTON TEA PARTY

In 1773 Boston, a group of Massachusetts's colonists disguised as Mohawk Indians boarded three British tea ships. In an act of patriotic defiance, they dumped 342 chests of tea into the harbor. This midnight raid, that became widely popular and pivotal to championing the cause of "No taxes without representation" came to be known as the "Boston Tea Party." It was a political movement in protest of the British Parliament's Tea Act of 1773, a bill designed to save the faltering East India Company by greatly lowering its tea tax and granting it a virtual monopoly on the American tea trade. It reminds me of some of the current one-sided trade deals, like NAFTA, our politicians in Washington have been signing into law to please the globalists in both parties.

The low tax allowed the East India Company to undercut even tea smuggled into America by Dutch traders, and many colonists viewed the act as another example of taxation tyranny by the British parliament. When three tea ships, the *Dartmouth,* the *Eleanor,* and the *Beaver,* arrived in Boston Harbor,

The genesis of the American Revolution can be traced back to the issues of taxes.

the colonists demanded that the tea be returned to England. After Massachusetts Governor Thomas Hutchinson refused, patriot leader, Samuel Adams, organized the "tea party" with about 60 members of the Sons of Liberty, his underground resistance group. The British tea dumped in the Boston Harbor by Samuel Adams' Sons of liberty was worth several thousands of dollars.

The British Parliament was outraged by the blatant destruction of British property. In retaliation, the British Parliament enacted the Coercive Acts of 1774. This very harsh legislation closed Boston to merchant shipping and established formal British military rule in Massachusetts. The Coercive Acts also made British officials immune to criminal prosecution in America. Can you imagine a British official raping one of the daughters of the colonists, only to be declared "untouchable?" The legislation passed by the British Parliament also required colonists to house British troops in their homes. Talk about a complete invasion of privacy. Was all of this turmoil and bloodshed over a cup of tea? No, my friend, the tea was just the symptom of a system of government that practiced taxation tyranny, by taxing its subjects while refusing to give them proper representation in the application of tax policy.

TAXES: THE DIVIDING LINE

It's clear from just reading the history of the American Revolution that taxes have always been at the center of America's resurgence or its decline. Paying taxes is as sure as death if you live in America, unless you want to buy yourself a "jail ministry" through tax evasion. Over the years of studying, the progressive left's political world-view versus that of fiscal conservatives, the dividing line between these two political worldviews comes down to how they see the role of government and taxes in society.

For the progressive left, government is the solution to the people's needs and the medium for achieving the coveted goal for a "socialist utopia." In such a worldview, it's the federal government's job to take care of the people. This being the case, more government welfare programs are required to sustain the ever-growing population, after all they are all entitled to it. In order to fund these ever-growing government welfare programs, more money is needed, which inevitably leads to the need to raise taxes. In the minds of the progressive left higher taxes are never a problem, because after-all the top 1% of income earners in America have more money than they deserve. These 1% percenters have lots of money. Why?

The progressive left will tell you, it's because they have not been paying their fair share of taxes, even though there is no-one in the progressive left's political "la-la-land" who knows the actual measure of "fair share." If I ever had an audience with President Obama, I would like for him to answer the question, "What's your measure for fair share?" This kind of thinking is the reason taxes almost always go up when progressives take the reins of power. Taxes also have to go up under progressives because it is one of the sure means for effecting wealth redistribution.

While people on government welfare programs always do well under progressive administrations, their policies always stifle the free market and demoralizes free-thinking-independent entrepreneurs (small business owners) by over burdening them with higher taxes and unending government regulations. On the other hand, fiscal conservatives see government's role as more of a passive-aggressive bystander whose job is to simply safeguard the safety and security of the marketplace so free-spirited American entrepreneurs can take advantage of the forces of the free market to either win big or lose; without too much government interference.

Since fiscal conservatives know, the issue of risk in a free market system is tilted against the small business owner who is putting up the capital, they hate to see government add to the risk by charging higher taxes. In their view, the person who risks the most ought to keep most of what they earn when the free market rewards their risk. They don't deserve to be robbed by a federal government that thinks their hard-earned money is better spent on taking care of welfare recipients. Consequently, under conservative administrations, taxes tend to go down. U.S. History also shows that when both Presidents Kennedy (a Democrat) and Reagan (a Republican) lowered taxes there was an economic boom in America and millions of new jobs were created.

DONALD TRUMP'S TAX VISION

✓ *Reduce taxes across-the-board, especially for working and middle-income*

Americans who will receive a massive tax reduction.

- ✓ *Ensure the rich will pay their fair share, but no one will pay so much that it destroys jobs or undermine our ability to compete.*
- ✓ *Eliminate special interest loopholes, make our business tax rate more competitive to keep jobs in America, create new opportunities and revitalize our economy.*
- ✓ *Reduce the cost of childcare by allowing families to fully deduct the average cost of childcare from their taxes, including stay-at-home parents*

It's not surprising therefore, that Donald Trump is getting some of his inspiration for his bold tax policy from the examples set by Presidents John F Kennedy and Ronald Reagan. What is truly exciting about his proposed tax plan is that it's born out of having spent most of his life creating a business empire, which employs thousands of people. He knows firsthand the unnecessary government regulations and taxes that he had to wrestle with in order to stay afloat. Having a President in the White House, who actually had to balance budgets, pay taxes and meet payroll is quite refreshing indeed. Below is an excerpt from his campaign website of a speech he made about his proposed tax plan.

Taxes are one of the biggest differences in this race. Hillary Clinton – who has spent her career voting for tax increases – plans another massive job-killing $1.3 trillion-dollar tax increase. Her plan would tax many small businesses by almost fifty percent. Recently, at a campaign event, Hillary Clinton short-circuited again – to use a now famous term – when she accidentally told the truth and said she wanted to raise *taxes on the middle class.*

I am proposing an across-the-board income tax reduction, especially for middle-income Americans. This will lead to millions of new good-paying jobs. The rich will pay their fair share, but no one will pay so much that it destroys jobs, or undermines our ability to compete. As part of this reform, we will eliminate the Carried Interest Deduction and other special interest loopholes that have been so good for Wall Street investors, and people like me, but unfair to American workers.

Tax simplification will be a major feature of the plan. Our current tax code is so burdensome and complex that we waste 9 billion hours a year in tax code compliance.

> *Business Tax: The Trump Plan will lower the business tax rate from 35 percent to 15 percent, and eliminate the corporate alternative minimum tax. This rate is available to all businesses, both small and large, that want to retain the profits within the business. It will provide a deemed repatriation of corporate profits held offshore at a one-time tax rate of 10 percent.*[1]

I don't know anyone in business that doesn't think the United States' corporate taxes are too high. So much so, that many American companies, like Apple, are keeping billions of dollars in revenue generated overseas, in offshore accounts. We will talk more in the next chapter about President-elect Trump's pledge to help these companies repatriate these profits back to the United States. Suffice it to say 35% corporate tax is just too high. This high-level taxation punishes job creators and demoralizes others who want to enter the field of play. This is in addition to the enormous and burdensome government regulations, on both the federal and state level, that businesses have to deal with to avoid hefty penalties. It is no wonder our highly taxed corporations find outsourcing of jobs to other countries quite enticing. Doing business in the United States is not easy and President Obama just loaded the private sector with more regulations; never mind the ones added by the progressive-left leaning EPA.

5

REPATRIATE PROFITS

To Launch this chapter we start with a simple "word study." What does the word, repatriate mean? According to the website dictionary.com, the word means:

1. To bring or send back (a person, especially a prisoner of war, a refugee, etc.) to his or her country or land of citizenship.
2. (Of profits or other assets) to send back to one's own country.

Can you believe that in a country (USA) where over 76 million Americans are unemployed or under-employed there is trillions of dollars held in offshore accounts by American corporations trying to come home? Imagine that you are fighting a war that you know is winnable if you can only get more troop reinforcements; what would you do if you discovered there was a battalion of U.S. Navy seals across the border? If you have any sense you would do whatever it takes to get those Navy seals across the border so you can win the war. How would you feel, if you lost the war, not to mention the lives of thousands of your soldiers, because the reinforcements didn't come due to the fact some bureaucrats in Washington were having an ideological argument about balancing the rules of engagement with their lopsided ideas about diplomacy. As a general who just wants to win a winnable war you'd be very upset.

Make no mistake; the United States of America is in a real war. It's a war for economic survival at a time when China is becoming an economic behemoth. It's naïveté on our part to think the Chinese are our friends. To the Chinese, the United States of America is a necessary evil on its way to global political and economic domination. Why else do you think that the trade deals between the between America and China are so one-sided? The United States does not tax goods coming from China into the USA but American companies face stiff tariffs when they try to ship their products into Mainland China. This is why President-elect Donald Trump promised to renegotiate our trade deals with China when he was running for the White House. But this is a subject for another chapter.

BRING THE MONEY HOME!!!

Under President Obama we have gone from $10 to $19 trillion in debt. The fiscal breaking point is $20 - $21 trillion- we are that close! We are propping up America by printing Monopoly money (called quantitative easing) and setting ourselves up to become a banana republic with triple digit runaway inflation like Venezuela or Zimbabwe. Wall Street is a bubble right now, much like the housing market of 2008. The only

> *difference is that we can't bail ourselves out again.*[1]

It's breathtaking! How did one President add more debt to the United States' national deficit than all previous U.S. presidents combined? Is Obama just a reckless spender or was there a hidden agenda in the reckless spending under his eight-year term? My money is on the latter. To unmask Obama's invisible but deliberate agenda for the reckless spending, we must once again turn to the book, *Rules For Radicals*, by a man who helped influence and forge Obama and Hillary's political ideology, Saul D. Alinsky. In the book, *Rules for Radicals,* he gave his followers milestones of achievement on the road to imposing massive wealth redistribution and socialism on a nation. In Saul D. Alinsky's view, capitalism is the cancer that must be terminated before progressives can achieve a socialist utopia. Below are two milestones or pillars of Saul D. Alinsky's strategy for fundamentally transforming a nation:

> *Poverty: Increase the poverty level as high as possible, poor people are easier to control and will not fight back if you are providing everything for them to live.*
>
> *Debt: Increase the debt to an unsustainable level. That way you are able to increase taxes, and this will produce more poverty.*

The United States' national deficit is truly at a tipping point of $19 trillion and counting. So you ask yourself, why would the progressive left not want to repatriate trillions of dollars belonging to American companies in offshore accounts? Alinsky gives us the answer. You need both debt and poverty to lead a capitalist state in the direction of socialism and social justice. This is why the progressive left is never in a hurry to pay off the national debt. Repatriating anywhere between $2 to $5 trillion dollars of American money in offshore accounts into the United States would overwhelm the progressive left's march towards socialism and reverse some of the gains they have already made. Why else would anyone propose charging American companies hefty taxes just to repatriate their profits?

MAKING AMERICA RICH AGAIN

This wealth that's parked overseas, nobody knows how much it is, some say it's $2.5T, I have people that think it's five trillion dollars. We'll bring it back, and it'll be taxed only at the rate of 10% instead of 35%. And who would bring it back at 35%? Obviously nobody, because nobody's doing it. By taxing it at 10% rather than 35%, all this money will come rolling back into our country. ***Donald Trump***

When President-elect Donald J Trump was running for the White House he made it clear that it is impossible to make America great again if we fail to make America rich again. Money is power and becoming a debtor nation is not the best way to retain that power. Solomon, one of the richest and wisest kings who ever lived said, *"The borrower is a slave to the lender."* Perhaps this is why China has very little respect for the United States of America because we owe it too much money.

LOWERING THE BUSINESS TAX

When you are Donald Trump and have spent much of your life in the private sector building a business empire, there's very little you don't know regarding why American companies are keeping their profits in offshore accounts in other countries. He probably has some of his own profits generated from his iconic hotels and casinos in other nations stuffed in offshore accounts as well. He knows the only thing that's keeping this massive amount of money from American companies in offshore accounts is the toxic and expensive business environment in the United States of America.

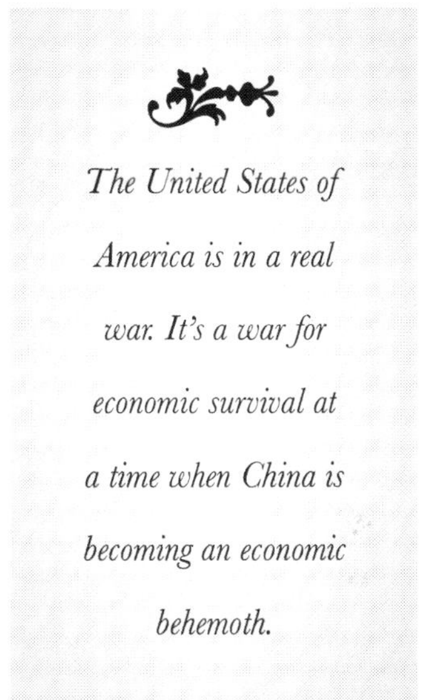

The United States of America is in a real war. It's a war for economic survival at a time when China is becoming an economic behemoth.

I'm almost sure that he has been in conversations with the other business tycoons and CEOs of mega corporations who would love to repatriate their profits to the U.S.A. But in fairness to their investors and shareholders it makes much more business sense to leave the money in offshore accounts accruing interest. Why would they bring their hard-earned profits to the United States under the current tax code? Would you bring your hard-earned money from offshore if you know that you will be hit with a 30-35% tax as soon as the money crosses the border?

Trump's proposal on how to incentivize American corporations to repatriate their profits is not born out of political expediency but from the crucible of expedience.

As it stands, the Trump plan will lower the business tax rate in the United States from 35% to 15%, and eliminate the corporate alternative minimum tax. This rate is available to all businesses, both small and large, that want to retain the profits within their business. Here is the kicker: The Trump plan will provide a repatriation of corporate profits held offshore at a one-time tax rate of 10 percent. Now how is that for incentive? Would you rather pay a one-time 10% repatriation fee or 35%? You don't have to answer I know what you would rather pay. If President Trump follows through with what he promised as a candidate to repatriate profits from offshore, America will be well on its way to becoming rich again.

6

BUILD BORDER WALL

And He has made from one blood every nation of men to dwell on all the face of the earth, and has determined their pre-appointed times and the ***boundaries (borders)*** *of their dwellings,* ***so*** *that they should seek the Lord, in the hope that they might grope for Him and find Him, though He is not far from each one of us; for in Him we live and move and have our being, as also some of your own poets have said, 'For we are also His offspring.' Acts 17:26-28 (Emphasis mine)*

BORDERS or boundaries between nations go as far back as the days of Nimrod, the first black global leader. After God intercepted the building of the Tower of Babel, he separated the people into different languages and ethnos (tribes). These different ethnos quickly turned into the League of Nations. The physical barriers that separated them came to be known as boundaries or borders. It can be inferred from the above scripture that the whole concept of borders between nations originates from the very heart of God. Since God is "love," one can argue that borders or boundaries are an act of love. Taking this thought further, we can say, "borders protect love and also facilitate love." Consider for a moment that if there were no implied borders or boundaries, morally, legally or spiritually, what is to stop me from having sex with my best friend's wife?

If there were no implied or stated boundaries, why would my friend be upset with me or his wife, if he found us in bed together? Even members of the gay community expect boundaries to be respected in their sexual relationship with their partners. This is why members of the gay community fought tenaciously to get the right to marry under the U.S. Constitution. Why? It is because they wanted to create a constitutionally protected boundary or border to safeguard their partnerships. If borders don't mean anything, why even bother putting up such a fight?

The borders that God allowed to develop between nations also protected the sovereignty of each new nation or ethnos. These borders also became a way of preserving the unique culture and language of the people group within those boundaries. The concept of borders is also the basis for the concept of property and ownership. How can you ever ascertain the issue of property and ownership, in a borderless society? If the line or border between my yard and my neighbors means nothing, why should I even bother to pay for a title deed stating my ownership of my piece of real estate? What if I came home one night and my neighbor had decided to dig up my yard to plant roses? Upon confronting him for his actions, he responds, "Why are you being such a bigot?" Suppose my offending neighbor is black and I am white; does standing up for the *integrity or sovereignty of my yard mean that* I am a racist? Obviously, the answer of most reasonable people would be off course not! So why is Donald Trump a racist bigot for wanting to seal and protect our porous southern borders?

THE OPEN SOCIETY

The progressive left's inability to understand the above analogy is beyond me. Progressive utopia is a borderless and open society. Their grandeur idea for America is a United States without borders. What bothers me though, is the hypocrisy of the progressive left. Like some sleazy used car salesman, they are trying to sell us on the merits of a borderless America while they isolate themselves in multimillion-dollar mansions protected by high-fortified walls.

The concept of borders is also the basis for the concept of property and ownership. How can you ever ascertain the issue of property and ownership, in a border-less society?

Have you driven through Beverly Hills or Malibu, lately? The number of open society liberal movie stars who live behind thick brick walls will shock you. Whoever said, "What's good for the goose is good for the gander," has never met Hollywood liberals. Try to crash one of Beyoncé or George Lopez's private parties in the name of open borders and see if their highly paid security guards will allow you an entrance. You will be lucky if you don't end up in jail for trespassing.

Which begs the question, what piece of real estate is more important to protect, the private property of a movie star or the sovereign state of the United States?

THE FAILING BORDERLESS EU

As I stated earlier, the utopia of the progressive left is a borderless society, which is simply a symptom of their internal hatred for the principle of divine restraint, whether morally, legally or spiritually. In the creation of the European Union, they seemingly got their first win. The next giant trophy to fall to their vision for an open and borderless society was the United States of America. They know that as America goes so goes the rest of the world. For a short while the EU seemed to be flourishing under an open society mandate. However, like anything driven by liberal socialist policies the honeymoon didn't last long. Cracks began to quickly emerge in the failing borderless society called the EU.

As one would expect, open borders started attracting a massive wave of illegal immigrants from the Middle East, Africa, China and India. They have begun to slowly overwhelm the internal economic, moral, and social structures of the European Union. Many members of the EU were enthused by the idea of being able to drive to any country within the EU without requiring a passport or going through an immigration checkpoint. What they did not account for is that radical Jihadists from terrorist organizations such as ISIS and Al-Qaida would also use this same freedom to spread terror across this open society. One of the masterminds behind the Paris terrorist attacks that killed over 130 people in France, escaped capture by simply driving to Belgium. It was months before he was captured. How is that for open borders?

The EU experiment also seemed to work beautifully because rich countries like the United Kingdom and Germany were footing most of the bill for maintaining this massive open society. However, when most Brits began to see that there were areas of London the police were afraid to go into because Sharia law controlled these areas they started realizing that they were slowly losing their country to foreigners. When a London court convicted a known Muslim terrorist, only to have his conviction overturned by bureaucrats in Brussels, they knew they had reached a tipping point. Suddenly they started longing for power to control their borders to protect their national sovereignty. The majority of Brits began to rally to take their country back behind the likes of Nigel Farage, a vocal leader of the UK Independence Party, who argued for the merits of national sovereignty. His arguments mobilized a nation that was beginning to wake up to the horrors of a border-less society, chief among them- cultural extinction!

THE BRIT EXIT!

I will never forget where I was on the day of the Brit Exit. I was in Germany. All the pundits on TV pontificated, saying it would never happen. There was no way the EXIT vote was going to beat the REMAIN vote. British Prime Minister, David Cameron was so confident that his side of the argument (remain a borderless society) was going to prevail. He was so confident in the

REMAIN vote prevailing that he was the one who actually encouraged the vote on this historic referendum to go ahead. All the polls that night had the REMAIN vote prevailing easily and most British news anchors did not even attempt to hide their intellectual contempt for Brit Exit proponents like Nigel Farage and Boris Johnson.

I went to sleep that night believing that the REMAIN vote had taken the night. Boy, was I wrong! When I woke up and turned on the TV, I was shocked to discover that a last minute surge of the Brit EXIT vote had actually overthrown the REMAIN vote in what sent shock waves in the political and media establishment in of all Europe. The stunned expression on many of the news anchors was priceless. They were just coming to terms with the fact that the pollsters where wrong! The polls had not taken into account Brits who had never voted before. They too knew they were rapidly losing their country to the open borders society.

Republican Presidential candidate Donald Trump was the only politician running for office who predicted that the Brit Exit vote would prevail. The media in both the U.S. and in Europe had laughed at him, while calling him a buffoon and political novice. Once everything was said and done, he was the only U.S. politician who had seen it coming. It was very clear to me, that if you put it to a VOTE the majority of Americans and Europeans don't want open borders.

ANGELA, WHAT HAVE YOU DONE?

When Angela Merkel's government decided to unilaterally admit about

1,000,000 Syrian refugees without establishing a proper vetting system, she mortgaged the future and security of the German people. ISIS and Al-Qaida had already warned that their militants would infiltrate these refugee populations. How stupid is this? Why would a savvy politician like Chancellor Merkel do such a stupid thing? Maybe it's her desire to atone for and cleanse her deep-seated guilt over Germany's Nazi history. Mark my words; *the German people will be paying in blood for many years to come because of Angela Merkel's misguided compassion.*

Look at Germany now; since they admitted these un-vetted Muslim refugees from Syria, occasional acts of terror and the pervasive rape of German women by Muslim men is quickly becoming the new norm in Angela Merkel's Germany. What about the recent Muslim refugee from Syria who just drove a truck onto a Christmas Market in Berlin that was patronized by thousands of innocent and unarmed Germans? Thirty-five German citizens were killed and hundreds more sustained serious bodily injuries. How is this good payoff for open borders?

In an article written by Victoria Friedman for Breitbart, Chancellor Merkel doubled-down on her nonsensical open-border-weak-on-vetting immigration policy, which is sure to doom the Germany people to a future patronized by unending acts of terror. Most importantly most of the Muslim Syrian refugees she imported to Germany will never assimilate into the German culture. Soon there will be sections of German cities that will be governed by Sharia law in which the German police will have no jurisdiction. Just ask the Brits!

In her New Year's speech, Chancellor Angela Merkel affirmed that her government will win the fight against terrorism with compassion and denied that her open-door mass migration policy, which directly brought terrorists to Germany, was wrong.

In the federal chancellor's New Year address to Germany, Merkel asserted that the terror attacks committed by Islamist migrants in Würzburg, Ansbach, and recently at a Christmas market in Berlin were not attacks on Western civilisation but an attack on 'refugees' and Germany's *willkommenskultur* ('welcome culture'). She stated terrorists "mock [the willingness of Germany to help] with their deeds [acts of terrorism], like they mock those who really need and deserve our protection."

> *Adding that it is "particularly bitter and repulsive" when terrorist attacks are committed by migrants, Merkel pushed back against criticism of her unwavering commitment to mass migration, saying that Germany will fight the "hatred" of terrorism with "humanity" and "unity."* [1]

BEWARE: OPEN BORDER RINOS AHEAD

On December 28, 2016 the conservative news site Newsmax released a report courtesy of the Associated Press, about the challenges president-elect Trump is having trying to win the support of some open-border Republicans like Speaker Paul Ryan and Senator Jeff Flake of Arizona.

Donald Trump's pledges to deport undocumented immigrants and build a U.S.-Mexico border wall-helped fuel Republicans' surprising election victories, but they now face growing challenges from fellow party members. Three Republican senators are working with Democrats to shield about 750,000 young undocumented immigrants from deportation if Trump cancels a 2012 order from President Barack Obama that let them stay in the U.S.

> *Lawmakers want to ensure that children who were brought here by their parents, through no fault of their own, are able to stay and finish their education and continue to contribute to society,» said Republican Senator Jeff Flake of Arizona. Republicans Lindsey Graham of South Carolina and Lisa Murkowski of Alaska are joining him on a measure drafted by the No. 2 Democratic leader, Dick Durbin of Illinois, that will be introduced after the new Congress convenes Jan. 3. Trump›s campaign was largely powered by his get-tough stance on immigration. A Pew Research Center poll in August found that 79 percent of Trump voters want a border wall, compared with 38 percent of all registered voters.* [2]

Trump supporters cannot afford to relax their vigilance to help President Trump "Make America Great Again." When it comes to the issue of illegal immigration, the progressive left also has sympathizers on the Republican side of the aisle. Both sides of the political divide benefit from leaving our southern borders open for illegal immigrants from undeveloped countries. For RINOs (Republicans In Name Only), illegal immigration is a source of cheap labor for their conservative donor class. On the other hand for the progressive left, illegal immigration guarantees them an ongoing influx of a dependent, mostly uneducated immigrant population that they intend to turn into Democratic voters using government welfare programs.

Consequently, the stage is set for the showdown between President Donald Trump and the open-border society in both political parties. My fellow Americans who want to see our government finally enforce immigration laws and protect our southern borders, need to pick up the phone and call the offices of their congressional representatives each time they oppose the president on the issue of fixing illegal immigration.

I believe that President Donald Trump is going to need the help of the people who put him into office more than ever before. You and I know that the mainstream media will never warm up to President Donald Trump. They're just going to double down on attacking him like they did during his presidential campaign. They will begin to push the narrative that he is a racist bigot for trying to enforce immigration law.

TRUMP'S IMMIGRATION AGENDA

President-elect Donald Trump's immigration agenda was clearly laid out in a rousing speech that he made in Phoenix, Arizona, after he returned from a meeting with the president of Mexico. It was one of his boldest immigration speeches during the campaign season. Without any hint of political correctness the "Donald" confronted the problem of illegal immigration and open borders head-on. Below is an excerpt of this amazing speech. I believe that if president-elect Donald Trump does not allow open borders RINOs, like speaker Paul Ryan, to derail him in establishing his bold, sensible America-first-immigration-plan, we are going to see the resurgence of America.

Thank you, Phoenix. I am so glad to be back in Arizona, a state that has a very special place in my heart. I love the people of Arizona and, together, we are going to win the White House in November. Tonight is not going to be a normal rally speech. Instead, I am going to deliver a detailed policy address on one of the greatest challenges facing our country today: immigration.

I have just landed having returned from a very important and special meeting with the President of Mexico – a man I like and respect very much, and a man who truly loves his country. Just like I am a man who loves the United States. We agreed on the importance of ending the illegal flow of drugs, cash, guns and people across our border, and to put the cartels out of business.

We also discussed the great contributions of Mexican-American citizens to our two countries, my love for the people of Mexico, and the close friendship between our two nations. It was a thoughtful and substantive conversation. This is the first of what I expect will be many conversations in a Trump Administration about creating a new relationship between our two countries. But to fix our immigration system, we must change our leadership in Washington. There is no other way.

The truth is, our immigration system is worse than anyone realizes. But the facts aren't known because the media won't report on them, the politicians won't talk about them, and the special interests spend a lot of money trying to cover them up. Today you will get the truth. The fundamental problem with the immigration system in our country is that it serves the needs of wealthy donors, political activists and powerful politicians. Let me tell you who it doesn't serve: it doesn't serve you, the American people.

When politicians talk about immigration reform, they usually mean the following: amnesty, open borders, and lower wages. Immigration reform should mean something else entirely: it should mean improvements to our laws and policies to make life better for American citizens. But if we are going to make our immigration system work, then we have to be prepared to talk honestly and without fear about these important and sensitive issues.

For instance, we have to listen to the concerns that working people have over the record pace of immigration and its impact on their jobs, wages, housing, schools, tax bills, and living conditions. These are valid concerns, expressed by decent and patriotic citizens from all backgrounds. We also have to be honest about the fact that not everyone who seeks to join our country will be able to successfully assimilate.

> *It is our right as a sovereign nation to choose immigrants that we think are the likeliest to thrive and lourish here. Then there is the issue of security. Countless innocent American lives have been stolen because our politicians have failed in their duty to secure our borders and enforce our laws.*
>
> *I have met with many of the parents who lost their children to Sanctuary Cities and open borders. They will be joining me on the stage later today.* [3]

Trump's immigration speech left no room for any misunderstanding. If elected Donald J Trump was going to enforce existing immigration laws and protect our porous southern borders. His presidency would be the death nail in the coffin of open borders. Legal immigration with extreme vetting would take precedence over the open borders policies of previous administrations.

7

APPOINT CONSTITUTIONALIST JUDGES TO THE COURT

"We have a very clear choice in this election. The freedoms we cherish and the constitutional values and principles our country was founded on are in jeopardy. The responsibility is greater than ever to protect and uphold these freedoms and I will appoint justices, who like Justice Scalia, will protect our liberty with the highest regard for the Constitution. **Donald J Trump**

THE DEATH of justice of Anthony Scalia was a tipping point in the political dynamics of the 2016 presidential race. His death was a terrible blow for conservatives and evangelical Christians alike. In the meantime, his death was celebrated by the progressive left who saw him as an obstacle on the nation's highest court against their agenda to remake America according to their image. Justice Scalia's death also gave the Hillary Campaign and Democratic Super PACs a rallying cry for raising millions of dollars from their liberal donor class. Money poured in from progressives from New York to Hollywood, who were extremely confident Hillary would win by a landslide.

Hugh Hewitt makes this observation:

If Hillary Clinton wins, the Left gavels in a solid, lasting, almost certainly permanent majority on the Supreme Court. Every political issue has a theoretical path to SCOTUS, and only self imposed judicial restraint has checked the Supreme Court's appetite and reach for two centuries.

That restraint will be gone when Hillary Rodham Clinton's appointee is sworn in. Finished. This is not hyperbole. I have the advantage of having taught Conservative Law for 20 years, of having argued before very liberal appellate judges like Judge Stephen Reinhardt of the very liberal Ninth Circuit, of practicing with the best litigators in the land. I know what a very liberal Supreme Court means: Conservatism is done. It cannot survive a very strong-willed liberal majority on the Supreme Court. Every issue - EVERY issue - will end up there, and the legislature's judgments will matter not a bit.

> *Imagine the impact on religious liberty and free speech when courts with a liberal majority hear cases by the "Human Rights Campaign" - America's largest civil rights organization advancing lesbian, gay, bi-sexual and transgender equality.* [1]

GAME CHANGER!

What the progressive left failed to see and grossly underestimated is that the death of Justice Anthony Scalia was, in actuality, the worst thing that could've happened to Hillary's chances for becoming the first female president in U.S. history. For conservatives and evangelical Christians who had been sitting on the sidelines the death of Justice Scalia was a game changer! The death of Justice Anthony Scalia meant that conservatives and evangelical Christians in America had just lost a conservative judge on the Supreme Court who they could depend upon to thwart the progressive left's agenda to transform America into a godless society. As an evangelical pastor, this was also a tipping point for me. It was no longer about the off-the-cuff and sometimes offensive comments Donald Trump made on the campaign trail. It was now about the future of our constitutional republic. Many evangelical pastors were quite reluctant to vote for Donald Trump at the time.

Some Evangelical pastors were hoping and praying that either Marco Rubio or Ted Cruz was going to emerge the winner of the highly contested Republican presidential race. As fate would have it both Marco Rubio and Ted Cruz lost their presidential bid to Donald Trump. Once Donald Trump was declared the clear winner of the Republican presidential primaries, I began to see Evangelical pastors who did not want to vote for Donald Trump begin to slowly warm up to his candidacy. The issue of the vacancy on the nation's highest court was weighing heavily on their minds.

THE TIPPING POINT

The death of justice of Anthony Scalia was a tipping point in the political dynamics of the 2016 presidential race.

Once it became a two-way race between Hillary Clinton and Donald Trump many reluctant conservatives and Evangelical Christians knew that they could no longer afford to stay on the sidelines. For the most part, the death of Justice Anthony Scalia robbed them of such a luxury. The stakes for the presidential elections had just been raised a notch higher because of his death. Most conservatives and Evangelical Christians knew that choosing between a Supreme Court Justice chosen by Hillary Clinton or one chosen by Donald Trump, they would take their chances with the one chosen by Trump. Hillary definitely did not help herself in the presidential debates. In the last debate moderated by Fox News' Chris Wallace, Hillary Clinton's inability to condemn, or at least distance herself from, the barbaric practice of late-term abortions, which even some pro-choice Democrats do not like, terrified the last evangelical Christians who were sitting on the sidelines.

Hillary's refusal to answer whether she could see herself defending the life of an unborn child in the final month of a pregnancy exposed her as an extremist even for liberal pro-choice Democrats. Her husband, Bill Clinton, had outlawed late-term abortion during his administration. Sixteen years later, on national television with President Clinton seated in the background, his wife refused to take a stand against what is a very barbaric practice against the unborn, even for liberals. However, Donald Trump's moral clarity on this issue after Hillary stumbled and fumbled with the question, may have won him the presidency. I remember thinking that night after the debate, "Its over! His got this." Members of the biased mainstream media and highly paid political pundits on the left missed this pivotal moment when Hillary Clinton became candidate zero for most white evangelicals and some pro-life independents.

TRUMP'S POTENTIAL JUSTICES

I believe, it is Fox News' Sean Hannity that encouraged Donald Trump to go out of the gate and name the potential list of justices he would nominate to the Supreme Court. This was a totally brilliant idea. This was at a time during the campaign when some conservatives and evangelical Christians were sitting on the sidelines. Many of them were planning on staying home on the day of the election. After weeks of promising to do so, Donald Trump finally released the "A" list of potential justices he would appoint to the Supreme Court.

When conservatives, evangelical Christians and conservative news outlets saw the list of Donald Trump's potential justices to fill the vacancy on the Supreme Court they were extremely delighted. All of the men and women who were on his "A" list were Scalia types in their legal disposition. This helped to ease the reluctance of some conservatives and evangelical Christians who were having a difficult time warming up to Trump's candidacy. If President-elect Trump nominates a candidate for the Supreme Court from this list after he is sworn into office, conservatives and evangelical Christians who voted for him will feel vindicated.

DONALD J. TRUMP'S IDEAL JUSTICE

Taking the words directly out of the horse's mouth, below is President-elect Trump's ideal Justice. I will appoint…

> *Justices to the United States Supreme Court who will uphold our laws and our Constitution. The replacement for Justice Scalia will be a person of similar views and principles who will uphold and defend the Constitution of the United States.*

- *Defend the rule of law and the Constitution of the United States. Nobody is above the law.*
- *Uphold our freedoms, constitutional values and principles that our country was founded on.*
- *Protect our Constitutional liberties.*
- *Protect and defend the bill of rights, including the freedom of religion, speech, press and right to bear arms.*

In an era of activist judges, it's refreshing to know that Donald Trump is focused on nominating a justice to the Supreme Court who will just allow the Constitution to speak for itself. I can't wait to see who he will nominate to fill Justice Scalia's seat on the nation's highest court.

8

FIX INNER CITIES

There is something deeply hypocritical in a society that holds an inner-city child only eight years old "accountable" for her performance on a high-stakes standardized exam but does not hold the high officials of our government accountable for robbing her of what they gave their own kids six or seven years before. ***Jonathan Kozol***

THE STORY of America's inner cities is nothing short of an American horror show! Dilapidated buildings, broken school systems, badly damaged roads, broken bridges and the inhumane living conditions of America's inner cities are a stain on the soul of America. The inner cities of America are infested with drugs, prostitution, violence and the inescapable stench of poverty. Most of the population in America's inner cities is on welfare, surviving on government food stamps without an ineffective way of getting out of the vicious crutches of poverty that enslaves them. The poverty of America's inner cities creates other social vices, such as broken homes, raping of women, and addiction to alcohol as a means of numbing the pain ofliving in such hopelessness.

For many of the inhabitants of America's inner cities, which is mostly African-Americans, Hispanics and illegal immigrants the fight for survival leads many of its budding youth into a life of crime, drugs and for most of them an express ticket into the American justice system. Once many of these young lives are incarcerated for anything from petty crimes to more serious felonies, the prison system becomes a never-ending revolving door. Once you are labeled a felon in the U.S. you effectively become a de-facto citizen of the American prison system. The prison number they give you is your registry into this new nation. They control you when you are in prison or out of it. The United States of America accounts for 5% of the world's population and yet has 25% of the global prison population. Why? It's big business! It's the modern tool for cheap labor under the banner of rehabilitation. Don't get me wrong; I am not suggesting there should not be a prison system in America. God knows that there are serious offenders in society and they must be incarcerated to protect the law-abiding population.

When I first came to America in 1998, by divine providence I found myself living in Chicago. The Christian family that opened their home to me were African-American and they were part of the budding American middle class. They lived in a very fancy home in the south suburbs of Chicago. Naively I thought that all of America looked like their fancy home. I was very proud to be finally in the land of the free and the home of the brave. When I was asked by an African-American pastor to speak at his church in the inner city of Chicago I gladly accepted. But then he told me that his church was in the ghetto in Chicago. I couldn't wrap my mind around his statement because in my mind, "how could there be ghettos in the richest country on planet earth?" When we finally drove to his church we passed through the most dilapidated buildings I had ever seen, even by African standards. Many of the buildings were riddled with bullet holes. Trash was on every side of the road. African-Americans and an occasional Hispanic sat under corroded bridges drinking beer, with a hopeless stare in their eyes. The picture I saw was like a photo taken in Haiti after the devastating earthquake. But this was not Haiti; this was a ghetto in the Chicago heartland, a modern American city by anyone's standard. This city was the home of one of the most popular African-Americans in the world, Oprah Winfrey!

IT'S POLITICS!!!

Coming from a political family in Africa, I have always known that the problems of society are rooted in politics, because politics is the art of governance. I became obsessed with wanting to know the politics behind American ghettos. As an African-American I already considered myself a de-facto Democrat when I arrived in the U.S. I joined my fellow African-Americans in celebrating the presidency of William Jefferson Clinton with great fanfare.

I must admit I still have a love for President Clinton even though I now realize politically speaking I am a social conservative. As I researched the politics behind American's ghettos, I was shocked to discover that there was a common denominator. I discovered that with very little exception, Democrats governed the cities that had ghetto populations. The city of Chicago is a prime example of a Democratic stronghold. Your chances of winning political office as a Republican or Independent in the city of Chicago are very slim indeed. And yet the story of ghettos in Chicago has only grown worse. This discovery alone is one of the singular reasons that led me to begin to look for political solutions outside of the Democratic Party to the problems facing African-Americans. In addition, as a Christian I was already biased towards a biblical pro-life position, which violated the Democratic Party's pro-choice platform.

OBAMA'S LEGACY

In 2008 a young and very charismatic, black United States Senator from Illinois took the American political world by storm. His name was Barack Hussein Obama. When he launched his presidential bid, in Springfield, Illinois no one gave him much of a chance. Most thought that white America would never allow a black man to become President of the United States. Even optimistic political commentators didn't think that Americans were ready for a black President of the United States. Naturally, astute political pundits, both liberal and conservative, gave the odds of winning the Democratic presidential nominee to Hillary Clinton.

Race baiters in the African American community were out in full force prognosticating that "White America" had too much in-built racism to ever give a black Presidential candidate a fair shake. Boy, were they wrong!!! Everybody thought the favorite racehorse to win the presidency was then

Sen. Hillary Rodham Clinton who was 25 points ahead of Barack Obama in the presidential polls at the time.

Shortly after Senator Obama entered the presidential race, I went to sleep one night and God gave me a prophetic dream. I dreamt that Barack Obama was going to become President of the United States, not once but twice. I woke up and told my wife what the Lord had shown me. Even though I was quite concerned about some of the socialist rhetoric Senator Obama was advocating in his political rallies I actually attended one of his rallies in Dallas, Texas. I grew up in a socialist country where those same policies he was advocating had failed us miserably. For this reason, I was concerned with how he would govern once he became President of the United States.

I was born and raised in Zambia under a socialist president, Kenneth Kaunda, were I saw the horrors that socialist policies of big government, free healthcare, high taxes and free education can confer on the economy and any people group that embraces these policies. In Zambia during the 80s we went through everything that socialist Venezuela is now going through. We went through the complete collapse of the national economy as the government ran out of OPM (Other Peoples Money!) Unfortunately, after eight years of his presidency, President Obama has confirmed all my earlier misgivings about his socialist tendencies. Whether Democrats believe it or not, Obama has also presided over the colossal collapse of the Democratic Party nationwide. They have lost over 1000 political office seats across the country since he took office. Even though most Americans (myself included) personally admire Obama as a man, his policies have not fallen on an accepting audience.

HISTORY IS MADE!

However, this misgiving about Obama's socialist tendencies did not dampen my excitement about the historic implications of having the first black president in the United States of America. When President-elect Barack Obama was sworn in as the 44th President of the United States my eyes were glued to the TV. I must admit I was quite teary-eyed. As a black man who knows the history of struggle and bigotry that most people of color have endured in the last 200 years; the election of a black man as the head of state of the most powerful country on earth was no small matter. The majority of African-Americans no matter his or her political affiliation, had to pause for a second and bask in the historic moment. Without a doubt, American political and presidential history would forever be changed by the election of America's first black president. Even though I was teary-eyed, emotional, and excited at the election of America's first black president; I was also very proud of "White America." It was clear to me that there were not enough African American or Hispanic voters to elect America's first black president without the help of our Caucasian friends. I knew of many white Republicans who crossed party lines to elect America's first black President. The election of President Barack Obama was proof of how far the United States of America had come in terms of race relations.

Unfortunately, America's first black president is leaving the White

House without having done anything significant for African-Americans, economically speaking. Obama's America has produced more African-Americans living on food stamps than Bill Clinton and George Bush combined. The ghettos of America are far worse and still governed politically by Democrats. When President Obama was campaigning for the failed presidential bid of Hillary Clinton, he made the case that African-Americans needed to show up at the polls to preserve the legacy of his signature bill, Obamacare. Louis Farrakhan leader of the Nation of Islam chastised the President for these remarks. In his opinion the President's remarks were misguided because Obamacare was not his legacy. His legacy should have been the plight of his fellow African-Americans.

VOTES TAKEN FOR GRANTED!

Have you ever been taken for granted? It doesn't feel nice. You feel betrayed and used. This is the growing sentiment that I'm coming across among African-Americans. They're beginning to slowly question the value of their undying loyalty to the Democratic Party. What has it brought them? Poverty, food stamps, a broken justice system, and a perennial life on government welfare is not the reward for political loyalty African-Americans were looking for. The truth of the matter is that voting for Democrats for more than six decades without any real change for African-Americans is finally taking its toll. Let's be honest, Democrats running for office know they can always depend on the African-American vote to tip the scales in their favor. Most especially if they turn on the charm of identity politics, by labeling their opponents a racist even if there is no supporting evidence of it. But are Democrats taking the votes of African-Americans for granted?

When President Obama was campaigning for Hillary, he condescendingly said to African-Americans that he will consider it a personal insult to his legacy if they don't show up in droves and vote for Hillary, a woman who has done very little in her 30-year political career to advance the careers of people of color. Obama's tone generated a response from the Reverend Louis Farrakhan on a Sunday during the Men's Day program. Below is a transcript of that speech: (you can watch this sermon on YouTube)

> *"Your people are suffering and dying in the streets," of Chicago, so "you failed to do what should have been done." "It is time to let Republican presidential nominee Donald Trump do "what he wants to because he is not destroying your legacy.*
>
> *So you Democrats, you been in their party a long time. Answer me, what did you get? You got a president. He is worried about his legacy. You want Hillary to get in to protect your legacy because Trump said the minute he gets in, he is going to reverse the Affordable Care Act. Because that is your signature achievement. To show you how hateful the enemy is, he hates that you achieve what you did achieve. So he said I'm going to tear it up when I get in. So he don't want his legacy destroyed. Mr. President, let the man do, if he get in, what he wants to because he is not destroying your legacy. If your legacy is bound up in an Affordable Care Act that only affects a few million people and they are trying to make*

it really difficult for those of us who signed up, that's not your legacy."

He continued, "But I just want to tell you, Mr. President, you're from Chicago, and so am I. I go out in the streets with the people. I visited the worst neighborhoods. I talked to the gangs. And while I was out there talking to them, they said 'You know, Farrakhan, the president ain't never come. Could you get him to come and look after us?' There's your legacy, Mr. President. It's in the streets with your suffering people, Mr. President. And If you can't go and see about them, then don't worry about your legacy 'cause the white people that you served so well, they'll preserve your legacy. The hell they will. But you didn't earn your legacy with us. We put you there. You fought for the rights of gay people. You fought for the rights of this people and that people. You fight for Israel. Your people are suffering and dying in the streets! That's where your legacy is. Now you failed to do what should have been done."

WOMEN'S HEALTH OR LEGALIZED GENOCIDE?

I bet you many members of today's African-American community do not know who Margaret Sanger is. She was a die-hard Democrat and a popular speaker at gatherings of the infamous Ku Klux Klan. According to filmmaker, Dinesh D'Souza, *Margaret Sanger came up with an original proposal: let's prevent these useless people (**blacks**) from even existing. Let's stop them even before they are born. This was the whole point of "birth control," and it became one of the foundation* *stones of early progressivism. The progressives recognized the value of Sanger's cause. So did the leadership of the Democratic Party. If useless people aren't born, we don't have to segregate them, nor do we have to chase them down and kill them. People who don't exist can hardly pose a problem. For one thing, they can't vote Republican.* While it's true that today's Democrats do not hold these radical views about blacks, the favorite organization of progressives, i.e., Planned Parenthood, was founded by a woman who did. Margaret Sanger was a hard-core believer in eugenics, a practice that the Nazis also embraced to eliminate less desirable races, like the Jewish people.

In an article written by Jerome Hudson for Breitbart News, he reports on singer and TV personality, Nick Cannon's views on the subject of Margaret Sanger. I was actually surprised that Nick Cannon was this politically astute. Most importantly that he was bold enough to say what he said, while working in Hollywood.

Singer and TV personality Nick Cannon doubled down on his criticism of Planned Parenthood, saying the abortion provider was designed to "exterminate" black people.

"When you talked about Margaret Sanger, all the people who follow eugenics. It was all about cleansing," the America's Got Talent host said of Planned Parenthood's founder in a recent interview with DJ Vlad.

"Margaret Sanger said that she wanted to exterminate the negro race, and that she was going to use her organization as she founded to do so," Cannon continued. "It was more about the sterilization and where it comes to actual ethnic cleansing — where they actually said we want to get rid of a class of people a group of people. "Seventy-five percent of

them are all in the hood." "They like to label 'feeble-minded' or 'lower-class,' that's what they used in public. In private, they were talking about the black community," Cannon said.

> *The 36-year-old rapper-actor says the issue of abortion is more personal than political. "I'm pro-Nick because my mother did go to an abortion clinic to abort me," he said. "I don't feel like the government should have the right. I don't feel like any organization that makes money should have the right to tell a woman what she can or cannot do with her body." Cannon says while Planned Parenthood — like the government — does some good things, it should be held accountable for "all the negative things."* [1]

Have you ever driven through majority black or Hispanic neighborhoods? You will be shocked by how many Planned Parenthood clinics you will find in these inner cities, compared to upscale, predominantly white suburbs. Why are these abortion clinics located in majority black neighborhoods? Don't white people have just as much unprotected, out-of-wedlock sex as blacks do? So where are these abortion clinics in these upscale neighborhoods? Since Planned Parenthood is essentially a big business, it follows the marketing rules of all successful businesses; locations in close proximity to your target audience. As a black man, I often wonder how large and influential the black vote would be if our babies were not aborted in such astronomical numbers? African-Americans would be a more powerful voting block in the U.S.A if we kept all of our babies.

LET'S GIVE MR. TRUMP A CHANCE!

While some of my African-Americans friends might accuse me of being a sell-out, I want to implore the African-American community to give Mr. Trump a chance at repairing our broken inner cities. Whether some of you like it or not Donald Trump will be inaugurated as our 45th President on January 20th, 2017. Protest posters saying, "He is not my President" are not going to change the plight of our fellow African-Americans in the inner city as much as working with our new president will. Running into politically correct safe-spaces on politically correct college campuses is also not a strategy for moving forward. When President-elect Trump saved 1000 Carrier jobs in Indiana from going to Mexico, some of the people who got to keep their jobs were African-American and Hispanic.

Most past Republican presidential candidates easily conceded the African-American vote to the Democrats without putting up a fight. But Donald Trump was not comfortable with conceding the African-American vote. Unlike past Republican presidential candidates, he fought hard for the African-American vote, even when the media labeled him a white racist.

African-Americans saw the sincere effort he made to win their vote, so November 8, 2016 they gave him a wider margin of support for his presidency than they gave to John McCain and Mitt Romney. But Donald Trump won't be satisfied until he wins more African-American support over the next four years by doing more for inner-cities than any president, Republican or Democrat, before him. Below is an excerpt of candidate Donald Trump's appeal to African-Americans in a speech he made in Milwaukee, Wisconsin.

"I am asking for the vote of every African-American citizen struggling in our country today who wants a different future. It is time for our society to address some honest and very difficult truths.

The Democratic Party has failed and betrayed the African-American community. Democratic crime policies, education policies, and economic policies have produced only more crime, more broken homes, and more poverty.

Let us look at the situation right here in Milwaukee, a city run by Democrats for decade after decade. Last year, killings in this city increased by 69 percent, plus another 634 victims of non-fatal shootings. 18-29-year-olds accounted for nearly half of the homicide victims. The poverty rate here is nearly double the national average. Almost 4 in 10 African-American men in Milwaukee between the ages of 25-54 do not have a job. Nearly four in 10 single mother households are living in poverty. 55 public schools in this city have been rated as failing to meet expectations, despite ten thousand dollars in funding per-pupil. There is only a 60% graduation rate, and it's one of the worst public school systems in the country.

The story of America's inner cities is nothing short of an American horror show!

1 in 5 manufacturing jobs has disappeared in Milwaukee since we fully opened our markets to China, and many African-American neighborhoods have

borne the brunt of this hit.

To every voter in Milwaukee, to every voter living in every inner city, or every forgotten stretch of our society, I am running to offer you a better future. The Democratic Party has taken the votes of African-Americans for granted. They've just assumed they'll get your support and done nothing in return for it. It's time to give the Democrats some competition for these votes, and it's time to rebuild the inner cities of America – and to reject the failed leadership of a rigged political system.

> *I'm not part of the corrupt system. In fact, the corrupt system is trying to stop me. I've been paying my own way. The voters in the Republican Party this year defied the donors, the consultants, the power brokers, and choose a nominee from outside our failed and corrupt and broken system."* [2]

I heard from many of my African American friends who told me that they were deeply moved by Trump's speech and sincere appeal to African- American voters. They realized that it would have been so easy for him to have simply forgone the African-American vote as a lost cause. Instead they saw his determination to win their support. Both Mitt Romney and John Mc-Cain gave a lip service request for the African-American vote during their presidential runs. But Donald J Trump actually walked the streets of the inner cities of Detroit and Flint, fighting for the African-American vote. Its no wonder he got a bigger slice of this vote than John McCain and Romney.

9

ENERGY INDEPENDENCE

IT'S HIGH TIME America had a president in the White House who has enough gusto, gamesmanship, and the political will to finally arm wrestle away the EPA's choking hold on America's energy resources. The EPA has an ironclad chokehold on the American economy. The EPA has become the progressive left's special tool for remaking America into their image and likeness by using the environment. Under the guise of trying to protect the environment, the EPA maintains a very liberal view of the environment. Imagine how many projects would have produced billions of dollars in revenue, while creating thousands of jobs that where killed by the restrictive policies of the so-called Environmental Protection Agency.

When I first came to America, for the life of me, I could not understand why a super power nation sitting on vast oil resources, subjected itself and its citizens to a totalitarian organization such as OPEC and the EPA? OPEC is the Organization of Petroleum Exporting Countries and it was founded at a meeting on September 14, 1960, in Baghdad, Iraq by five founding members: Iran, Iraq, Kuwait, Saudi Arabia and Venezuela.

Let's face it; the member states of OPEC do not care about the United States of America or the welfare of its citizens. Does anyone remember the nefarious Hugo Chavez, late president of Venezuela? He had no love for the U.S.A and yet through OPEC he had the power to determine the price of oil for the United States. How crazy is this?

BACK TO THE EPA

How insane that our oil is coming from countries that believe America and Israel are the greatest threat to civilization.

As I began to do my research and educate myself on the politics of the United States of America, I began to discover just how vastly powerful the EPA really is. Take the keystone pipeline for instance; even though the majority of Americans, unions and members of both political parties supported it, the EPA and its environmental foot soldiers still prevailed. This was at a time when millions of dollars worth of studies had already shown that the pipeline would have minimal impact on the environment. Against the wishes of the majority of Americans, the Obama administration capitulated to the whims of the EPA and environmentalists on the progressive left. Thank God, President Trump will put the keystone pipeline back online and create thousands of good paying jobs.

FAKE GREEN ENERGY SOLYNDRA OR DRILLING?

Most Americans are not opposed to harnessing all forms of energy; they just don't want to be held hostage by the oil-producing nations of the Arab world. How insane that our oil is coming from countries that believe America and Israel are the greatest threat to civilization. Politics is truly stranger than fiction. The Obama administration, in the name of energy independence and the desire to harness solar energy, gave a $500 million federal grant to Obama donors to run a so-called "green energy" company called Solyndra. Solyndra was supposed to be a testament to the viability of solar energy over dirty oil. In the long run, it turned out to be just another legal loophole for Obama to pay off some of the donors who had contributed to his presidential campaign.

Solyndra went through the $500 million like a drunken sailor who had lost his mind. Within a couple years of Solyndra was bankrupt. What would have happened had this massive amount of money been given to a savvy businessperson from the private sector who invested the money in a sure thing – oil? In one of the worst cases of the far-left's crony capitalism, Solyndra was declared a failed venture, but the government never got any returns on the tax-dollars that were invested in this project. Ironically, while this outraged everyday Americans, the astronomical waste of federal tax-dollars was another play call from Saul D. Alinsky's, *Rules for Radicals*. Bankrupting a capitalist state like the U.S.A. through this kind of wasteful spending is permitted in Saul Alinsky's playbook if the endgame is to collapse the current system in order to replace it with a new system.

AN AMERICA FIRST ENERGY PLAN

When Donald Trump was running for office he did not mince his words in proclaiming his passionate support for the exploration of all forms of energy available to Americans. Candidate Trump criticized the United's States self-inflicted subjugation to OPEC. In the state of West Virginia where Hillary Clinton promised to put coal miners out of business, Donald Trump pledged his unwavering support for America's coal industry.

He was especially opposed to the destructive policies of the EPA that were designed to wipe out the coal industry. Let's not forget that President Obama's administration was very hostile to the coal industry. Trump promised that a Trump administration would pursue an all-options-are-on-the-table strategy for harnessing energy independence. This means that drilling on American soil for oil and natural gas would be an integral part of Donald Trump's administration. Below is an excerpt of Donald Trump's "America First Energy Plan" from his campaign website and in his own words.

> *Make America energy independent, create millions of new jobs, and protects clean air and clean water. We will conserve our natural habitats, reserves and resources. We will unleash an energy revolution that will bring vast new wealth to our country.*

- *Declare American energy dominance a strategic economic and foreign policy goal of the United States.*

- *Unleash America's $50 trillion in untapped shale, oil, and natural gas reserves, plus hundreds of years in clean coal reserves.*

- *Become, and stay, totally independent of any need to import energy from the OPEC cartel or any nations hostile to our interests.*

- *Open onshore and offshore leasing on federal lands, eliminate moratorium on coal leasing, and open shale energy deposits.*

- *Encourage the use of natural gas and other American energy resources that will both reduce emissions but also reduce the price of energy and increase our economic output.*

- *Rescind all job-destroying Obama executive actions. Mr. Trump will reduce and eliminate all barriers to responsible energy production, creating at least a half million jobs a year, $30 billion in higher wages, and cheaper energy.*

This America first energy plan as part of the governing philosophy of a Trump administration is just want the doctor ordered. I look forward for an American renaissance in the energy sector under a President who is not beholden to both OPEC and the EPA.

10

SAY IT! RADICAL ISLAM

"What exactly would using this label accomplish? What exactly would it change? Would it make ISIL less committed to try to kill Americans?" Obama said. "Would it bring in more allies? Is there a military strategy that is served by this? The answer is none of the above." ***President Barak Obama***

AFTER EIGHT years of the Obama-Clinton foreign policy, America is weaker on the international front than it has ever been. Do you remember when President Obama drew the infamous red line in Syria that he warned must never be crossed by the Assad regime? He was very clear that if the Assad regime used chemical weapons on its people the United States would come against him in full force. Sadly, this redline did not take a long

Obama's redline turned out to be some imaginary moving redline in his own head. It kept moving every time the Assad regime crossed it.

time to be crossed. I believe the Assad regime was anxious to test President Obama's resolve. They crossed the president's redline by killing some of their own people with chemical weapons. And what was our President's response? Subdued silence! Obama's redline turned out to be some imaginary moving redline in his own head. It kept moving every time the Assad regime crossed it.

For the life of me I still do not understand why President Obama failed to understand that when you're dealing with the kind of pervasive terrorism coming from the Middle East, labels do matter. How can you change anything if you are afraid to call the problem for what it is? How can you fight the crime of sex trafficking if you refuse to call the problem by its proper name?

President Obama did not understand that when you fail to call any problem by its actual name you effectively embolden it. You also create tactical confusion in the security protocols of your own security agencies when what they're fighting is not clearly defined. President Obama's argument was that saying radical Islam would only be used as a recruiting tool for the terrorists. Secretary Clinton agreed. This was absolutely nonsensical if it was not deadly.

THE ENEMY HAS A NAME

Even after 49 gays and lesbians were gunned down in cold blood by an avowed Muslim terrorist in Orlando, Florida, the President refused to call this an act of radical Islamic terrorism. Before the 29-year-old terrorist, Omar Marteen, continued with his killing spree, he took time to record his pledge of allegiance to the leader of ISIS. Even then the Obama administration and Hillary Clinton were terrified to call these serious acts of terror - radical

Islamic terrorism. Even peace loving Muslims whose religion is being hijacked by these jihadists know it's better for them when we differentiate them from the radical Islamic terrorists. A President Trump will not be afraid to call it what it is – radical Islamic terrorism.

Below are short excerpts and portions of the speech Donald Trump made on defeating terrorism that you will find very refreshing and direct. It leaves you with no doubt as to what the name of our enemy really is. It's an ideology rooted in a perverted version of Islam. It is radical Islamic terrorism. My barbers are all Muslim, but they are the very decent kind. I know, and so do most Americans, that when I say "Radical Islamic Terrorism" I am in no way suggesting that every Muslim on this planet is a terrorist.

We all know that is not the case because we can see on television that some of these radical jihadists are also blowing up fellow Muslims. But it's important, in the most consequential fight of our generation, to call the problem for what it is - terrorism. Under a Trump administration just giving members of law enforcement this type of clarity on the name of the enemy they are fighting will be quite revolutionary compared to the past eight years.

NEW SHERRIFF IN TOWN!

Thank you. It is great to be with you this afternoon.

Today we begin a conversation about how to Make America Safe Again. In the 20th Century, the United States defeated Fascism, Nazism, and Communism. Now, a different threat challenges our world: Radical Islamic Terrorism…

In June, 49 Americans were executed at the Pulse Nightclub in Orlando, and another

53 were injured. It was the worst mass shooting in our history, and the worst attack on the LGTBQ community in our history.

In Europe, we have seen the same carnage and bloodshed inflicted upon our closest allies. In January of 2015, a French satirical newspaper, Charlie Hebdo, was attacked for publishing cartoons of the prophet Mohammed. Twelve were killed, including two police officers, and 11 were wounded. Two days later, four were murdered in a Jewish Deli. In November of 2015, terrorists went on a shooting rampage in Paris that slaughtered 130 people, and wounded another 368. France is suffering gravely, and the tourism industry is being massively affected in a most negative way…

We cannot let this evil continue. Nor can we let the hateful ideology of Radical Islam – its oppression of women, gays, children, and nonbelievers

– be allowed to reside or spread within our own countries. We will defeat Radical Islamic Terrorism, just as we have defeated every threat we have faced in every age before.[1]

What a difference it will make on the most consequential fight of our time, the "fight against terror" to have a president in the Oval office, who is not afraid to name the enemy, we face. "Radical Islamic terrorism" is the name of the ideology and face of the enemy against western civilization. President-elect Trump has already made it clear he will not be afraid to take the fight to ISIS and Al-Qaida. Radical Islamic terrorism, like "fascism" before it, can and will be defeated, if we don't drown our frontline security agencies in the heavy wet blanket of political correctness.

11

EXTREME VETTING

WHAT'S WRONG with vetting people before you import them into your country? Would you take a homeless man from the street and bring him into a house full of little children without making sure he was mentally fit to be around your children? What if he was a deranged serial killer and he kills one of your children, while you slept? How would you feel when you realize that you are the one that opened the door to your house without knowing who you were inviting into your home? I am sure you would be devastated and remorseful. But that would not bring back your dead child.

Every day as we watch news from around the globe we are constantly reminded that we live in a very dangerous world. But nothing is more dangerous today than the ongoing threat of hard-core radical Islamic terrorism. Terrorism is real, devastating and a very present danger. At the risk of being labeled a racist bigot by some on the progressive left, the cancer of terrorism has one very distinct and common factor: 95% of the times, it is perpetuated by Muslim men or women, or foreign nationals who have been converted to this radical version of Islam. I am deeply aware that the majority of Muslims are peace-loving people and they too decry the scourge imposed on their religion by radical Islamic terrorists. In many instances these moderate, peace-loving Muslims are themselves victims of radical Islamic terrorism.

SAN BERNARDINO TERRORIST ATTACK

On December 2, 2015, 14 people were killed and 22 were seriously injured in a terrorist attack at the Inland Regional Center in San Bernardino, California, which consisted of a mass shooting and an attempted bombing. The perpetrators, Syed Rizwan Farook and Tashfeen Malik, a married couple living in the city of Redlands, targeted a San Bernardino County Department of Public Health training event and Christmas party, of about 80 employees, in a rented banquet room. Farook was an American-born U.S. citizen of Pakistani descent, who worked as a health department employee. Malik was a Pakistani-born lawful permanent resident of the United States. [1]

I was visiting with a friend of mine in Glendale, California when the San Bernardino terrorist attacks happened. Every major news network was broadcasting the developments live. It was a massacre, another terrorist attack on American soil. The perpetrators of the attack, Syed Rizwan Farook and Tashfeen Malik, a married couple living in the city of Redlands. When details of the terrorist attack began to emerge they only confirmed our worst fears and what we already know. Our immigration system is broken, our vetting system for both legal and illegal immigrants is almost none existent. Adding fuel to the fire, our over-the-top toxic culture of political correctness had silenced neighbors who suspected the Muslim couple was up to no good. When asked why they didn't report the suspicious behavior that they witnessed they said, "We were afraid of being accused of racism." I am sure these neighbors were traumatized by the aftermath; they probably blamed themselves for not sounding the alarm, even at the risk of being attacked by the guardians of our politically correct culture.

In the postmortem analysis of the terrorist attack, it was discovered that it was the wife who radicalized her husband. She came into the United States intent on committing Jihad. Her husband Syed Rizwan Farook actually traveled to Saudi Arabia where he married her to make it easy for her to get immigration papers into the United States. It was later discovered through her Facebook posting that Tashfeen Malik, had strong ties to terrorist networks long before she came to the U.S.A. How did the FBI and the United States border control at the airport not flag her before they issued her a green card? This is how inept and broken our immigration vetting system is. How many terrorist attacks against our citizens do we need to experience on American soil before we wake up to the sensibility of crafting a very thorough immigration vetting system?

TERROR IN BERLIN

On 19 December 2016, a truck was deliberately driven into *the* Christmas market *beside* Kaiser Wilhelm Memorial Church *at* Breitscheidplatz *in* Berlin.

The terrorist attack left 12 people dead and 56 others injured. One of the victims was the truck's original driver, Łukasz Urban, who was found shot dead in the passenger seat. The perpetrator was Anis Amri, a Tunisian *failed* asylum seeker. *Four days after the attack he was killed in a shootout with police near* Milan *in Italy. An initial suspect was arrested and later released due to lack of evidence.*

> *The Islamic State of Iraq and the Levant (ISIL) claimed responsibility for the attack, saying the attacker answered its calls to target the citizens of states that are fighting against it. ISIL released a video of Amri pledging allegiance to the terror group's leader.* [2]

In the warped view of the progressive left, there seems to an unspoken belief that immigrants are more important than citizens

Stories of terrorism in the German heartland such as this one were extremely rare just a decade ago. Thanks to Angela Merkel's insane decision to taken in 1,000,000 Syrian refugees without vetting them properly, Islamic jihad has arrived on the German shores. In her distorted progressive way of thinking Angela Merkel believes showing acts of compassion to Muslims by German citizens will win the terrorists over. Many on the progressive left here in America share Merkel's thinking. In their distorted world view, if the United States of America can just start being nice ISIS militants will drop their machetes and suicide vests. Are you kidding me? Take the case of Anis Amri, the Tunisian born asylum seeker, who ended up killing12 innocent Germans in a market patronized by hundreds of children. Didn't the German people show him love and compassion when they opened the doors to their country so he could find some refuge? How did he respond to the love and compassion of the German people? He killed 12 of them and injured hundreds more to honor his allegiance to ISIS. How many Anis Amri's are lying in wait among the millions of un-vetted Syrian refugees that Chancellor Merkel imported into her country? Since the Syrian refugees moved to Germany, the rape of white women by young Muslim men is rising at an alarming rate. Is this what open borders looks like? In the warped view of the progressive left, there seems to be an unspoken belief that immigrants are more important than citizens. Why else would they be angry with Donald Trump for insisting on implementing a much needed system of extreme vetting?

Believe me, whatever speeches Angela Merkel makes about the merits of being a welcoming, open-border society it will not bring back the 12 dead Germans. They paid the ultimate price for her socialist experiment. The families who lost a loved one to the terrorist attack, will always know their loved ones died because Merkel's government thought it was more important to be welcoming to Muslims than to protect its citizens by properly vetting the massive refugee population. Below is a rousing speech that President-elect Trump made while he was running for office. I cannot wait for this policy of extreme vetting to go into effect.

EXTREME VETTING

In a speech in Youngstown, Ohio, on Monday, Republican presidential nominee Donald Trump laid out his main immigration policy proposals, which included what he called 'extreme, extreme vetting'.

"To defeat radical Islamic terrorism, we must speak out forcefully against a hateful ideology that provides a breeding ground for violence and terrorism to grow," Trump said.

"We need a new screening test for the threats we face today—I call it extreme vetting. Our country has enough problems—we don't need more."

"We need a new screening test for the threats we face today—I call it extreme vetting. Our country has enough problems—we don't need more." "We should only admit into this country those who share our values and respect our people," Trump said.

In explaining his plan, Trump invoked the ideological screening test that the United States implemented during the Cold War, when the capitalist West was at odds with the communist Soviet Union.

> *"In addition to screening-out members and sympathizers of terrorist groups, we must also screen-out any with hostile attitudes or beliefs that Sharia law should supplant American law."*
>
> *"Those that do not believe in our Constitution will not be admitted... into our country," Trump said. Trump also attacked Democratic opponent Hillary Clinton's plan to increase immigration flows from various countries by as much as 550%, according to his campaign.*
>
> *"The size of immigration flows are too large to support adequate screenings."*[3]

Having President Trump in the White House will be like having a parent at home who wont take chances with the life of his or her children by allowing strangers who have not yet been vetted, to come over for a sleep over. Even though this is simple common sense, there seems to be very little room left for commonsense in much of today's politically correct culture.

12

SEND EDUCATION BACK TO THE STATES

"A Bible and a newspaper in every house, a good school in every district--all studied and appreciated as they merit--are the principal support of virtue, morality, and civil liberty."

Benjamin Franklin

Genius without education is like quick silver in the mine

Benjamin Franklin

Educate and inform the whole mass of the people... they are the only sure reliance for the preservation of liberty."

Thomas Jefferson

The best means of forming a manly virtuous, and happy people will be found in the right education of youth. Without this foundation, every other means, in my opinion, must fall."

George Washington

Learned Institutions ought to be favorite objects with every free people. They throw that light over the public mind, which is the best security against a crafty and dangerous encroachments on the public safety.

James Madison

IT IS CLEAR from observing the wisdom of America's founding fathers that our current education system is far removed from their highest ideals of having an educational system that protects the blessings of liberty, while infusing students with an unshamed patriotism towards the United States of America. Unfortunately, many of our college campuses today are havens for far-left activist professors whose primary passion has little do with educating our children as much as it is about indoctrinating them into a Saul-Alinsky type of worldview.

A worldview, which is of the opinion that America is what is wrong with the world and its history, its gallant history, is something to be ashamed of. And yet, these far-left progressive professors cannot show you in human history a government of the people by the people so divinely crafted like the United States of America. America's political and economic revolution is unrivaled in history: a revolution that has defended other countries freedom, produced more millionaires, inventors, scientists, educators, preachers and athletes more than any other nation.

In Saul D. Alinsky's *Rules for Radicals*, there are eight levels of control that must be achieved before the creation of a socialist state. One of the steps is:

> *Education: Take control of what people read and listen to; take control of what children learn in school.*

Who knowingly sends their children to college to be indoctrinated by far-left radicals into a vision of America that causes them to hate their country and request safe spaces each time their ideas are challenged? There is a definite need for reformation of the American educational system under a Trump administration. If President-elect Trump can break the monopoly the progressive left has established over education through their bureaucratic teachers' union and instead allow for more access to charter schools, the entire American educational system will change for the better.

It is so sad that Democrats are willing to sacrifice our children by keeping them trapped in failing public schools in order to shore up support among the politically powerful teachers unions. Most of these inner city public schools are, for all practical purposes, broken. They just sentence many of these little poor children in the inner city to a life of crime and failure. But there is always an exception to the rule, "Ben Carson's story" of pushing through failing inner-cities schools to achieve the American dream, quickly comes to mind.

TRUMP'S PICK

On Wednesday, November 23, President-elect Trump picked Betsy DeVos for U.S. Secretary of Education. Betsy is a Michigan philanthropist and education activist who has chaired the state's Republican party and helped advance a number of educational reforms, such as the expansion of private-school choice and the passage of Michigan's charter school law.[1]

By picking Betsy DeVos, who is very pro-charter schools, President-elect Trump is showing the American people that he is serious about keeping his campaign promises to reform education and break the monopoly of Teacher's Unions over America's public school system.

In his own words, here are some of Donald Trump's thoughts on education, with recent quotes first:

1. School choice: *"As president, I will establish the national goal of providing school choice to every American child living in poverty. If we can put a man on the moon, dig out the Panama Canal and win two world wars, then I have no doubt that we as a nation can provide school choice to every disadvantaged child in America." September 2016.*

2. Funding his school choice plan: *"If the states collectively contribute another $110 billion of their own education budgets toward school choice on top of the $20 billion in federal dollars, that could provide $12,000 in school choice funds to every single K-12 student who today is living in poverty." September 2016.*

3. Common Core: *"I have been consistent in my opposition to Common Core. Get rid of Common Core." February 2016.*

4. America's schools: "We need to fix our broken education system!" *February 2016.*

5. Local control of education: *"Keep education local!" February 2016.*

6. Government's role in education: *"There's no failed policy more in need of urgent change than our government-run education monopoly." September 2016.*

7. American education in an international context: *"We're twenty-sixth in the world. Twenty-five countries are better than us at education. And some of them are like third world countries. But we're becoming a third world country." June 2015.*

8. Higher education loans: *"A four-year degree today can be expensive enough to create six-figure debt. We can't forgive these loans, but we should take steps to help students.... There is no reason the federal government should profit from student loans.... These student loans are probably one of the only things that the government shouldn't make money from, and yet it does.... Those loans should be viewed as an investment in America's future." November 2015.*

9. The U.S. Department of Education: *"No, I'm not cutting services, but I'm cutting spending. But I may cut Department of Education." October 2015.*

10. Education spending: *"We're number one in terms of cost per pupil by a factor of, worldwide, by a factor of many. Number two is so far behind, forget it." January 2016.*

11. American history: *"I was listening to some Europeans once and they seemed to agree that Americans didn't seem to know their roots. Of course, their roots go back for many more centuries than ours and may be easier to decipher because many of us have ancestors from different countries. But it gave me a reason to think about what they said, and I realized in many cases they were right." March 2010.*

12. Comprehensive education: *"Comprehensive education dissolves the lines between knowing too much and knowing too little on a variety of subjects—subjects that are necessary for success." March 2010.*

13. Citizenship education: *"Public education was never meant to only teach the three R's, history, and science. It was also meant to teach citizenship. At the lower levels it should cover the basics, help students develop study habits, and prepare those who desire higher education for the tough road ahead. It's a mandate the public schools have delivered on since their inception. Until now." January 2000.*

14. Teachers' unions and politics: *"Our public schools have grown up in a competition-free zone, surrounded by a very high union wall. Why aren't we shocked at the results? After all, teachers' unions are motivated by the same desires that move the rest of us. With more than 85% of their soft-money donations going to Democrats, teachers' unions know they can count on the politician they back to take a strong stand against school choice." January 2000..*

15. Education and antitrust: *"Defenders of the status quo insist that parental choice means the end of public schools. Let's look at the facts. Right now, nine of ten children attend public schools. If you look at public education as a business—and with nearly $300 billion spent each year on K-through-twelve education, it's a very big business indeed—it would set off every antitrust alarm bell at the Department of Justice and the Federal Trade Commission. When teachers' unions say even the most minuscule program allowing school choice is a mortal threat, they're saying: If we aren't allowed to keep 90% of the market, we can't survive. When Bell Telephone had 90% of the market, a federal judge broke it up." January 2000.*

16. School safety and school learning: *"Our schools aren't safe, which is bad enough. On top of that, our kids aren't learning. Too many are dropping out of school and into the street life—and too many of those who do graduate are getting diplomas that have been devalued into "certificates of attendance" by a dumbed-down curriculum that asks little of teachers and less of students. Schools are crime-ridden and they don't* *teach." January 2000.*[2]

By picking Betsy DeVos, who is very pro-charter schools, the Trump administration will start off on a revolutionary path to transforming our failing and mostly bureaucratic educational system. There was a time it looked like the powerful and politically connected teachers union would finally send "charter schools" into extinction. Most owners of charter schools, especially Christian charter schools were very concerned about the growing and hostile regulatory policies of the Department of Education against privately owned charter schools. If Betsy DeVos, is confirmed by the Senate to become Trump's Secretary of Education, schools will become more about educating our children rather than indoctrination centers for the progressive left.

Who knowingly sends their children to college to be indoctrinated by far-left radicals into a vision of America that causes them to hate their country?

13

REDEFINE FREE AND FAIR TRADE

THE MAINSTREAM media, pollsters, democratic strategists and professional pundits did not see it coming. They couldn't see that their favored candidate of choice, Hillary Rodham Clinton, was headed into a perfect storm. The perfect storm was the result of the backlash against years of Democratic and Republican led one-sided trade deals that were allowing multinational corporations to ship American jobs overseas. Many pundits and the mostly biased political media were very sure that the blue-wall of democratic leaning swing states such as Wisconsin, Michigan and Pennsylvania would hold.

Boy, were they wrong! On the other hand Donald Trump knew that the story of the "forgotten man" in America extended to blue-collar white Democrats, also known as Reagan Democrats. This blue-collar white working class had been left behind to wallow in the joblessness left by the loss of thousands of manufacturing jobs to China. They were left hopelessly unemployed, compliments of the globalists in both political parties.

Their problems were further compounded by the open border policies of Democrats and RINO-republicans, who were forcing them to compete with illegal immigrants for left over jobs. While the Washington elites in both parties were being wined, and dinned by lobbying firms representing foreign governments, the people of Wisconsin, Michigan and Pennsylvania were suffering.

For many of them they couldn't place a finger on what went wrong. But they knew that something was seriously wrong. What happened to their jobs? Where did they go? How were they going to feed their families and put their children through college? These questions were like twisters in the minds of these blue-collar Democrats and some independents. All they knew was that Washington; D.C. politicians no longer spoke up for them. When Donald Trump identified, and pinpointed with razor sharp accuracy, the source of their troubles – bad trade deals, he quickly won their support. The silent majority was longing to be heard. Every time Donald Trump was having a rally in the swing states of Pennsylvania, Wisconsin and Michigan he railed passionately like a broken record against bad trade deals such as NAFTA, which was signed by President Bill Clinton, and the infamous TPP that President Obama and Secretary Clinton were championing. He blamed the problems of the people of Pennsylvania, Wisconsin and Michigan on these nonsensical one-sided trade deals and the crowd rewarded him with thunderous cheers.

He reminded them of the good old days, when Michigan was at the center of the industrial revolution. It was the utopia of all American industrial cities that boasted of millions of well-paying jobs generated by the very robust car manufacturing plants in the Motor City. Fast-forward to 2016; Detroit, Michigan was a ghost town. Some suburbs in Detroit look like a picture taken out of war-torn Syria. Unemployment was looming on every corner. Some of the blue-collar white Democrats in the audience were lamenting their shrinking pay, ever fearful of losing more of their jobs to other countries. Donald Trump continued to rail against these one-sided trade deals every time he was in the swing states: states he campaigned in quite often, while Hillary barely campaigned there having made the assumption they were already hers for the taking.

The mainstream media didn't see the Trump-train plowing through Pennsylvania, Wisconsin and Michigan because of their very biased coverage of his candidacy. Having chosen sides (Hillary's), they failed to appreciate the genius of what Trump was doing. Consequently, they failed to see what he was seeing: the silent, telltale signs of a growing underground revolution. On the other hand, the average blue-collar Democrat in these economically hard-hit swing states heard him loud and clear. Most importantly they agreed with him. He also convinced them not to expect the same people (the ruling political class) who rigged the system in the first place to be the ones who fixed it. Washington, D.C. was broken and corrupt; it was in desperate need of a fresh face, with bold solutions. Trump assured the masses he was that man- their messenger.

TRADE DEFICITS

When Donald Trump begun to share the raw data behind America's trade deficits with China, Mexico and Japan. Everyday Americans hearing these astronomical numbers for the first time were outraged. How could our government allow such ridiculous deficits to exist? Why did they agree to these lopsided trade agreements in the first place? "The United States of America has a trade deficit with China of over $500 billion a year." Trump declared. "It has an annual trade deficit with Mexico of over $50 billion dollars. It also has an annual trade deficit with Japan of about $65 billion a year."

The more Donald Trump went through these numbers the more enraged the crowds became. Voters in the swing states of Pennsylvania, Wisconsin and Michigan got a very clear picture about the evils of these one-sided trade deals the United States was entertaining. Nevertheless, as the newly awakened silent majority they could do something about it. November 8, 2016, they could come out in full force to voice their displeasure with our broken political system by voting for a political outsider. Below is a short excerpt of President-elect Donald Trump's vision for negotiating fair trade deals that benefit the American people and bring back jobs to the United States (donaldjtrump.com).

DONALD J. TRUMP'S VISION FOR FREE TRADE

Negotiate fair trade deals that create American jobs, increase American wages, and reduce America's trade deficit.

Donald J. Trump's 7 Point Plan To Rebuild the American Economy

by Fighting for Free Trade

1. Withdraw from the Trans-Pacific Partnership, which has not yet been ratified.

2. Appoint tough and smart trade negotiators to fight on behalf of American workers.

3. Direct the Secretary of Commerce to identify every violation of trade agreements a foreign country is currently using to harm our workers, and also direct all appropriate agencies to use every tool under American and international law to end these abuses.

4. Tell NAFTA partners that we intend to immediately renegotiate the terms of that agreement to get a better deal for our workers. If they don't agree to a renegotiation, we will submit notice that the U.S. intends to withdraw from the deal. Eliminate Mexico's one-side backdoor tariff through the VAT and end sweatshops in Mexico that undercut U.S. workers.

5. Instruct the Treasury Secretary to label China a currency manipulator.

6. Instruct the U.S. Trade Representative to bring trade cases against China, both in this country and at the WTO. China's unfair subsidy behavior is prohibited by the terms of its entrance to the WTO.

7. Use every lawful presidential power to remedy trade disputes if China does not stop its illegal activities, including its theft of American trade secrets - including the application of tariffs consistent with Section 201 and 301 of the Trade Act of 1974 and Section 232 of the Trade Expansion Act of 1962.[1]

They couldn't see that their favored candidate of choice, Hillary Rodham Clinton, was headed into a perfect storm.

Ever since Donald Trump became president-elect he is sending very clear signals that the day of one-sided-trade-deals that ravage American jobs is over. He has made it clear every U.S. trade deal with other nations is up for renegotiation. These trade deals will be put through a measuring cylinder called "the America first policy." The fact that many giant U.S. corporations like Ford are now announcing that they will be canceling the construction of a new $1.5 billion plant in Mexico is quite telling. U.S trade deals are about to change radically and for the betterment of the American worker.

14

REMEMBER THE FORGOTTEN MAN

You know, to just be grossly generalistic, you could put half of Trump's supporters into what I call the basket of deplorables. Right? The racist, sexist, homophobic, xenophobic, Islamaphobic -- you name it. And unfortunately there are people like that. And he has lifted them up. He has given voice to their websites that used to only have 11,000 people -- now 11 million. He tweets and retweets their offensive hateful mean-spirited rhetoric. Now, some of those folks -- they are irredeemable, but thankfully they are not America." ***Hillary Rodham Clinton***

WHO SAID SPEECHES don't matter? Hillary Rodham Clinton, arguably the favored front-runner of the 2016 presidential race, lost the election and the chance to be America's first female president because of a speech. Most likely, in any other election cycle she would have gotten away with it. Just not this one! This was the "Year of the Forgotten Man." This was the year (2016) when Americans on both sides of the political divide were sick and tired of the elitism of the ruling class. Even though Democrats and the mainstream media ignored them, the telltale signs were everywhere. How else do you explain why Hillary almost lost the Democratic presidential nomination to an avowed socialist (Bernie Sanders), except for a biased DNC and super-delegates who stacked the deck against "Cool Bernie?" It was the year of the outsider and Democrats hedged their bets on a total insider.

Without a doubt, Hillary Rodham Clinton was a card-carrying member of the ruling class. She was what you would call a member of the Washington elite and political establishment. Perhaps this is why she never saw it coming - the Trump train! She never saw the possibility of losing to a loudmouth outsider like Donald Trump. Most importantly she never discerned the viral affect her "basket of deplorables" comment would have on the conscience of the American electorate. Her speech had the effect of pouring gasoline on the fire of an already contentious presidential campaign.

THE PROBLEM WITH BUBBLES

They say, *"The problem with living inside a bubble is that you forget about the people outside the bubble."* Consequently, you also forget how fragile bubbles are. They are called bubbles for a reason, they can bust at a moment's notice.

I would like to know the name of the over-paid speechwriter in the Hillary campaign who wrote or added those fateful words in her speech. Those words above any other cost her the entire election. For a $1.2 billion-dollar presidential campaign no words were more deadly than Hillary Clinton's "basket of deplorables." Her "basket of the deplorables" comment became the rallying cry for members of the forgotten man up to the day of the election. If the American people did not know how members of the political ruling class thought of them behind closed doors- now they knew. They were deplorable! Donald Trump knew instinctively that "the basket of deplorables" comment is just what the doctor ordered. The comment allowed him to separate himself from the Washington elite and once again remind ordinary Americans that they were about to go to the polls in the year of the outsider. In a gift that just kept on giving, Secretary Clinton had just reminded them (ordinary voters) that they, like Donald Trump, were also outsiders!

She never discerned the viral affect her "basket of deplorables" would have on the conscience of the American electorate.

SILENT MAJORITY AWAKENS

In an article written by the Washington Times, June 1 2016, they reported how Donald Trump was summoning the winning mantras of past U.S. presidents like Richard Nixon and the great Ronald Reagan.

Of the many smart moves Donald Trump has made during his campaign, one of the most impactful was his appropriation of Mr. Nixon's phrase. At a campaign rally last July in Phoenix, he said, "The silent majority is back, and we're going to take our country back."

After that, "the silent majority" appeared on Trump campaign placards, waved by thousands at his rallies. (He has also successfully appropriated President Reagan's 1980 slogan "Let's Make America Great Again." Both phrases appeal to the countless Americans who feel their country and its historic, unique greatness have been lost to radicalism and other diseases of the pathological left.)

> *An open question is whether, after decades of assault by the left, there is still a "great silent majority" left in America. Or have the radicals succeeded in turning those who believe in the founding principles of limited government, individual freedom and traditional values into the minority? The answer may be unclear for now. But Mr. Trump is banking on the continued existence of the majority — while at the same time working to reconstitute it for the 21st century.*[1]

There is absolutely no more powerful force both in life and politics like the silent scream of someone who suddenly demands to be heard. The problem with silent screams is that you do not hear them until it's too late. For the longest the American people on both sides of the political divide were trampled upon and simply ignored by the ruling political class. They watched in silence as their political leaders in Washington, D.C. kept passing legislation that did not reflect the interests of the people that sent them to Washington. In silence, they watched as their political leaders made one-sided trade deals with globalists who shipped American jobs to other countries.

For many of them their calls of desperation to their congressmen or senators went unanswered. It was as though they do not even exist. Slowly but surely it dawned on them that they had no voice in the current political system championed by the political establishment of both political parties. Year after year they suffered in silent frustration, feeling hopeless and desperate. For many of them they placed their hopes in the presidential run of the young, handsome, African-American senator from Illinois with oratory skills to die for. His hope and change message was quite refreshing for a silent majority long forgotten. Maybe the silent majority had finally found a politician who was going to do right by them.

When Obama's hope and change message turned into a nightmare and his progressive agenda morphed into the pursuit of far-left policies, the breakdown of traditional values, plus the remaking of America, the silent majority begun to revolt. When Obamacare was finally passed into law, their president promised them that the health care plan would never raise their insurance premiums or cause them to lose their doctors. He broke both promises.

It was in this environment where the electorate shared a collective consciousness of abandonment by the ruling political class that a loudmouthed outsider in the name of Donald Trump found an audience. An audience that no longer believed that career politicians were the only ones capable of fixing their problems. For the most part this silent majority now knew with certainty that career politicians were much of the problem. And such the platform was laid for the entrance of a complete outsider. Donald Trump's amazing instinct for the mood of the silent majority was borderline prophetic.

I AM YOUR VOICE

Donald Trump quickly established himself as the lone voice of the silent majority. In speech after speech, rally after rally, he told thousands of his supporters who stood in line for hours to hear him speak, "I am your voice." "I am your messenger." "I will go to Washington and fight for you." "Believe me." "I am an outsider, I am not part of this broken and corrupt Washington political system." "We cannot trust the very people who broke and rigged the system to fix it for us."

The silent majority, listened, cheered and some even cried. It was not just his speeches or his lack of political correctness that moved them, they genuinely felt his sincerity. They knew he was a billionaire (he reminded them constantly) but oh boy did he feel like one of them. When they left his rallies, they were politically charged. For many of them this was the first time they were going to be voting for a political candidate. His words, "I am your voice. I am your messenger. Believe me. I'm one of you. I'm an outsider and I'll go to Washington and fight for you" were ringing in their head as they drove back home. Donald Trump's campaign was no longer just his campaign: it had suddenly become *theirs*. They were going to vote no matter what. The pollsters did not see them coming. They were the hidden Trump vote – America's silent majority.

WHO DOES A THANK YOU TOUR?

I was living in the United States when President Bill Clinton won the

White House for a second term by defeating Senator Bob Dole. There was no "thank you" tour that followed to thank the voters who had reelected him. When George W. Bush was elected President after a contentious recount debacle in Florida there was no "thank you" tour to honor the voters that put him in power. When President Barack Obama was voted into office in a landslide, there was no "thank you" tour on behalf of the voters who put him in power. Then there was Donald Trump!

As soon as he won the presidential elections he quickly announced that he was going to be holding "Thank You" tours in some of the swing states to thank his supporters for putting him in the White House. It was clear that President-elect Donald Trump had not forgotten, the forgotten men and women of America who put him in the White House. I'm almost sure future presidential candidates will copy this strategy. What a way to reconnect with voters after they have already voted. The "thank you tours" also served to remind him why he ran for office in the first place. It was to be the voice, champion and fighter for the silent majority. The forgotten man would be forgotten no more. If President Donald Trump does not forget his commitment to the silent majority, we will see him follow-through on campaign promises he made that are designed to "Make America Great Again."

AMERICA'S FORGOTTEN VETERANS

In my humble opinion there is no forgotten man like our precious veterans. There are no persons that we owe our sincere gratitude to more than the veterans of our Armed Forces. They are the reason the United States of America is still the *home of the brave and the land of the free.* In a world filled with terrorism, pirates, and rogue dictators, freedom has many enemies. Without the self-less sacrifice of our men and women in the Armed Forces the enemies of liberty would easily cross onto our shores to destroy our freedom. Unlike the career paths many of us chose, these men and women chose to put their very lives on the line to defend the freedoms we take for granted.

Sadly, there is no population of Americans that are more disrespected by our broken political system than our veterans. Just look at how the Veterans Administration treats our veterans with impunity. The VA's attitude and treatment of veterans should show us everything we need to know about our out-of-touch-political establishment. It is no wonder many of our veterans are committing suicide at an alarming rate. Who wouldn't?

After giving your all to serve your country, the least you can expect is decent treatment when you return home from the battlefield. But to return to mistreatment and dishonor at the hands of the same government that sent you into war must be depressing. Thankfully, from the moment Donald Trump announced his presidential bid he made the issue of taking care of our veterans one of his primary campaign slogans. Since he became President-elect he has not changed his tune. He has announced major changes at the VA for the sake of our veterans. Below is Trump's vision of the Veterans Administration under a Trump administration.

DONALD J. TRUMP'S VISION

Ensure our veterans get the care they need wherever and whenever they need it. No more long drives. No more waiting backlogs. No more excessive red tape. Just the care and support they earned with their service to our country.

- *Support the whole veteran, not just their physical health care, but also by addressing their invisible wounds, investing in our service members' post active duty success,*
- *Transforming the VA to meet the needs of 21st century service members, and better meeting the needs of our female veterans.*
- *Make the VA great again by firing the corrupt and incompetent VA executives who let our veterans down, by modernizing the VA, and by empowering the doctors and nurses to ensure our veterans receive the best care available in a timely manner.* [2]

Many Veterans of the U.S. armed forces went out on November 8th, 2016 and voted for Donald Trump. Many of them knew that they had finally found a politician who would go into the Oval office and become their biggest champion. The days of having many of their fellow veterans dying in long lines waiting to see a doctor at the VA would soon come to an end under a Trump administration. Its clear that Trump's stint at a military academy gave him a deep-seated empathy for men and women in the military. Its time for a president who will honor our sacred duty to take care of those among us who have sacrificed the most for the freedoms we enjoy.

15

ABOLISH THE CULTURE OF POLITICAL CORRECTNESS

IN AUGUST 1971, I came into this world kicking and screaming, like all babies do. I was born in Zambia in what was then a socialist state moving rapidly towards communism. When I was old enough to understand and appreciate the prevailing political climate in the country I was born in, I was terrified. Speaking in hushed tones, my parents told me in no uncertain terms that I had to be very careful not to voice any political dissent with the government of Kenneth Kaunda.

As I grew older the more I became aware of the suffocation of free speech. As a matter of fact, many political dissidents disappeared in the night, never to be seen again after either criticizing the president's policy or disagreeing with a government minister. After a while you got the message, no free speech allowed! Free speech was quickly surrendered in exchange for a politically correct collective consciousness that we will do and say everything our socialist president wanted to hear. This silent obedience to a totalitarian state became the measure of good citizenship.

As I grew older and began to study about the United States, I became intoxicated with the idea of living in a country where citizens were guaranteed freedom of speech in the Constitution. When I watched American news networks allow guests with different political views and opinions appear on their TV shows, I was amazed. I found myself thinking, "What country is this?" In my country, if I criticized our president on television, I knew I would get a visit from the intelligence service and either got tortured or disappeared altogether.

When I finally moved to the United States in 1998, I was so thrilled. I had finally arrived in the one country on earth where I could say whatever was on my mind without the fear of violent or economic retribution. I am sad to say that the America of 2016 is beginning to feel more like the Zambia of 1980. The wet blanket of political correctness fueled by the liberal-left is having a choke hold on the most important freedom the founding fathers ever gave us for posterity. Below are some of the quotes from patriotic Americans from both sides of the political divide about now they all valued the freedom of speech.

> *"I disapprove of what you say, but I will defend to the death your right to say it."*
>
> **— S.G. Tallentyre, *The Friends of Voltaire***

> *"I may not agree with you, but I will defend to the death your right to make an ass of yourself."*

— ***Oscar Wilde***

"Censorship is to art as lynching is to justice."

— ***Henry Louis Gates Jr.***

"If freedom of speech is taken away, then dumb and silent we may be led, like sheep to the slaughter."

— ***George Washington***

"Whoever would overthrow the liberty of a nation must begin by subduing the freeness of speech."

— ***Benjamin Franklin, Silence Dogood, The Busy-Body, and Early Writings***

WE ARE ALREADY THERE!

"Once a government is committed to the principle of silencing the voice of opposition, it has only one way to go, and that is down the path of increasingly repressive measures, until it becomes a source of terror to all its citizens and creates a country where everyone lives in fear."

— ***Harry Truman***

It's sad to say that we are already there at Harry Truman's precipice! How prophetic was President Harry Truman? Was he looking in the face of God when he made the above statement? Compliments of the liberal-left, we have arrived at this juncture in American political discourse that

Harry Truman feared. We have arrived at that dangerous juncture where the mainstream news media, college professors, safe-space seeking millennials and Hollywood's liberal-left are dangerously committed to the principle of silencing the voice of opposition. How else do you explain the behavior of a restaurant in Hawaii that refuses to serve Trump supporters, even if it hurts their bottom-line?

How else do you explain why Hollywood movie stars banded together to intimidate electoral college electors not to vote for the man the people had elected in a landslide? And what was the reason they advanced for their undemocratic behavior? They did not agree with Donald Trump's views. In other words, Donald Trump was the voice of the opposition they couldn't stand. So they had to make sure he is silenced, even if it means disfranchising 62 million Americans who voted for him. According to Harry Truman, once you reach this point there is only one way for this to go - the creation of a country where everyone lives in fear. *"Once a government is committed to the principle of silencing the voice of opposition, it has only one way to go, and that is down the path of increasingly repressive measures, until it becomes a source of terror to all its citizens and creates a country where everyone lives in fear."*

DR. BEN CARSON

One of my favorite candidates in the 2016 Republican Presidential race was the soft-spoken Dr. Ben Carson. While he was running for the presidency my loyalty was divided between him and Donald Trump. I stumbled on

Dr. Carson's amazing story because of my love for movies and actor Cuba Gooding Jr. I watched Cuba Gooding Jr, do an amazing performance as the legendary neurosurgeon in the movie *"Gifted Hands"*. I may have cried a couple of times during the movie. After watching the movie, I became a die-hard fan of Dr. Ben Carson. I bought every book that he has ever written.

But it was Dr. Ben Carson's amazing speech at the national prayer breakfast that gave me the language for dealing with the wet blanket of political correctness that I had been dealing with as a black conservative. I was amazed by his boldness, because he delivered this speech in the presence of President Obama. Below is a short excerpt of that amazing speech, which may also explain the attraction that Dr. Ben Carson has for our President-elect.

> *You know, I'm reminded of a very successful young businessman, and he loved to buy his mother these exotic gifts for Mother's Day. And he ran out of ideas, and then he ran across these birds. These birds were cool, you know? They cost $5,000 apiece. They could dance, they could sing, they could talk. He was so excited, he bought two of them. Sent them to his mother, couldn't wait to call her up on Mother's Day, "Mother, Mother, what'd you think of those birds"? And she said, "They was good." [laughter] He said, "No, no, no! Mother, you didn't eat those birds? Those birds cost $5,000 apiece! They could dance, they could sing, they could talk!" And she said, "Well, they should have said something." [laughter] And, you know, that's where we end up, too,*

if we don't speak up for what we believe. [laughter] And, you know, what we need to do — [applause] what we need to do in this pc world is forget about unanimity of speech and unanimity of thought, and we need to concentrate on being respectful to those people with whom we disagree.

And that's when I believe we begin to make progress. and one last thing about political correctness, which I think is a horrible thing, by the way. I'm very, very come — compassionate, and I'm not never out to offend anyone. But pc is dangerous. Because, you see, this country one of the founding principles was freedom of thought and freedom of expression. and it muffles people. It puts a muzzle on them. And at the same time, keeps people from discussing important issues while the fabric of this society is being changed. And we cannot fall for that trick. And what we need to do is start talking about things, talking about things that are important.

I want you to do yourself a favor, go to YouTube and search for this amazing speech by Dr. Ben Carson at the national prayer breakfast. After listening to it whether you are liberal or conservative who cares deeply about freedom of speech you will develop a hatred for political correctness. I was held spellbound by his speech. It clearly outlined why the descent

Free speech was quickly surrendered in exchange for a politically correct collective consciousness.

of the American society into the cesspool of political correctness will be the undoing of the great American experiment. I believe that hatred for the toxic climate of political correctness that has been choking the free speech of everyday Americans may be one of the underlying factors, why some Americans voted overwhelmingly for a politically incorrect candidate like Donald Trump. Speaking at the Republican national convention in Cleveland, Dr. Ben Carson made another impassioned speech against the festering culture of political correctness in America. Below is a short paragraph from the speech.

> *Thank you, thank you, thank you everyone.*
>
> *I want to thank you all for that very warm welcome. I have to start out by saying one very important thing: I'm not politically correct. And I hate political correctness because it's antithetical to the founding principles of this country and the secular progressives use it to make people sit down and shut up while they change everything. It's time for us to stand up and shout out about what we believe in.*
>
> *You know, I devoted my career to studying and operating on the human brain. This remarkable organ defines our humanity. It gives us the ability to not only feel and observe, but to reason. When we elect a president, we need to use that power of reasoning to look at their history, their character, what kind of people they really are. It's all the difference in the world for us. And it is gonna be so critical right now. We must resist the temptation to take the easy way out and to passively accept*

what is fed to us by the political elite and the media because they don't know what they're talking about and they have an agenda.

GOD'S WRECKING BALL AGAINST THE PC POLICE!

Someone once told me that God has an amazing sense of humor. Just when it looked like the chokehold of political correctness would completely extinguish the flames of freedom of speech, God sent us his wrecking ball. On June 16, 2015 Donald Trump entered the race for the White House. He came down the escalator and announced his candidacy for the Presidency of the United States at his New York residence, the iconic Trump Tower. His announcement speech sent shockwaves in the political world. The mainstream media, both liberal and conservative were quick to brand him a "dead on arrival" candidate because of the politically incorrect speech that he had just given on national television. In an America where we have become accustomed to politicians lying to us by telling us what they think we want to hear, it is almost unheard of to have a political candidate be as blunt about what he or she thinks and believes.

I remember watching news anchors and commentators on CNN, MSNBC and Fox News who were completely shocked by Trump's tone. "Did he honestly call Mexicans rapists and drug dealers?" The news anchors asked incredulously. In their emotional overreaction to Trump's speech, the biased mainstream media did not accurately report what he actually said. He did not call Mexicans rapists or drug dealers. Instead he said that the Mexican government was sending rapists and drug dealers across our southern border even though he acknowledged that some of the people coming across the border were decent and peace-loving people. Republican presidential candidates like Jeb Bush who was the actual front-runner at the time were quick to join the chorus of the mainstream news media condemning Donald Trump. However, the reaction to Trump speech in the heartland of America was very different from the sophisticated news anchors in New York. To everyday Americans, Donald Trump's speech was refreshing, truthful and without any trace of the customary Washington BS!

During the Republican presidential primaries, I asked many people, including evangelical Christians why they were so captivated by the candidacy of Donald Trump. In almost every case they were quick to acknowledge that Donald Trump was not the perfect candidate. They knew he was flawed in many ways but for them he represented a much-needed departure from the toxic culture of political correctness that was muffling the free speech of so many everyday Americans, especially conservatives or evangelical Christians. People told me they were beginning to get afraid of their own shadows. When they saw how the liberal-left managed to silence the use of the word "Christmas" during Christmas they knew that if they did not put up a fight they would also lose their freedom to worship freely.

They began to realize that if the heavy wet blanket of political correctness could take away their constitutionally guaranteed right to freedom of speech what is to stop it from coming after their freedom of worship? For many white and even black evangelical Christians their support for Donald Trump was neither blind nor misguided. They simply saw in Donald Trump an American warrior who was willing to fight for traditional American values that were slowly being taken away by the drumbeat of political correctness. This is also the reason why many evangelical Christians showed up at the polls and voted overwhelmingly for Donald Trump. They were not just voting for Donald Trump, they were also voting for the end of freedom-stifling political correctness.

TWEETING HIS WAY AROUND THE MSM

Having watched the failure of the McCain-Palin and Romney-Ryan presidential campaigns Donald Trump learned his lesson pretty quickly. He realized that the failure of both of these presidential campaigns could be traced directly to the biased reporting of the mainstream media. He quickly realized that in the toxic culture of political correctness a Republican candidate can never hope to win the White House by playing the game of the mainstream media and the liberal-left.

John McCain and Mitt Romney both capitulated to the drumbeat of political correctness. They thought that by playing the game of the mainstream media they would get more media attention. Desperate for free and positive press they kissed the rings of the prophets of political correctness on the liberal-left. But the truth of the matter is that the mainstream media is very biased politically in favor of Democratic candidates. Donald Trump decided to tweet his way around the mainstream media. He had quickly sized up the mainstream media and realized that they were the priests and priestesses of the temple of political correctness. He knew he would never get a fair shake if he depended on them to report the truth against their favored candidate, Hillary Clinton. He also correctly discerned the mood of the American people, particularly conservatives and evangelical Christians who were tired of the toxic culture of political correctness. Perhaps this is why he was deliberately politically incorrect even when he did not need to be. Just to make a point.

Now as President-elect the "Donald" is already continuing with his tweeting ways. He is definitely not showing signs that he is going to give up his twitter account even as President of the United States. In the meantime, the same biased and lying mainstream media that was colluding with the Hillary Clinton campaign is now saying that his tweeting is not presidential. The reason they're saying this is because the mainstream media cannot stand having a politician especially the President of the United States, bypass them as the primary means of communicating with the American people.

Rush Limbaugh recently said that Trump is tweeting because he does not trust the mainstream media to report him correctly and he doesn't want anything to get between him and the American people. So, he's going directly to the American people and telling them exactly what he thinks. But most importantly, President Trump intends to use Twitter to prove the utter uselessness of the mainstream media and by so doing finally break the chokehold of political correctness the MSM has unleashed on the American people. Fortunately for Trump and all Trump supporters, the liberal-left is in great denial about why Hillary lost the election. They are so busy blaming the Russians or insulting Trump voters, they have not done an effective postmortem analysis of why Hillary Clinton lost to Donald Trump. Consequently, they don't realize just how much the Trump vote was not as much a vote for Trump as it was a vote against political correctness. Thus, they are bound by their own denial and their liberal biases to repeat the same mistakes they made with the election of 2016. They'll continue to rave-up the dying drumbeat of political correctness and thus ensure a second term for President Trump in 2020. As for me I can only say to President Trump, tweet, tweet and we will re-tweet!

16

JOBS, JOBS, JOBS!

YOU DIDN'T HAVE to wait long if you ever went to a Trump rally before you heard him say, "I will be the greatest job president God ever created." The crowd would cheer him on. I heard him say it, during a Trump rally I attended during the Republican primaries. I knew from the conviction in his voice that he meant every word. During the presidential debates when he was debating Hillary, Trump never changed his mantra. He kept pushing the point that we're losing American jobs to Mexico, China and other nations, because of one-sided trade deals. Below is a speech the he gave on "Jobs and the Economy" at the New York Economic Club.

TRUMP'S AGENDA ON JOBS & THE ECONOMY

Thank you for the opportunity to speak with you.

Today, I'm going to outline a plan for American economic revival – it is a bold, ambitious, forward-looking plan to massively increase jobs, wages, incomes and opportunities for the people of our country. My plan will embrace the truth that people flourish under a minimum government burden, and it will tap into the incredible unrealized potential of our workers and their dreams. Right now, 92 million Americans are on the sidelines, outside the workforce, and not part of our economy. It's a silent nation of jobless Americans.

Look no further than the city of Flint, where I just visited. The jobs have been stripped from this community, and its infrastructure has collapsed. In 1970, there were more than 80,000 people in Flint working for GM – today it is less than 8,000. Now Ford has announced it is moving all small car production to Mexico.

It used to be cars were made in Flint and you couldn't drink the water in Mexico. Now, the cars are made in Mexico and you can't drink the water in Flint. We are going to turn this around. My economic plan rejects the cynicism that says our labor force will keep declining, that our jobs will keep leaving, and that our economy can never grow as it did once before.

We reject the pessimism that says our standard of living can no longer rise, and that all that's left to do is divide up and redistribute our shrinking resources. Everything that is broken today can be fixed, and every failure can be turned into a great success.

Jobs can stop leaving our country, and start pouring in. Failing schools can become flourishing schools. Crumbling roads and bridges can become gleaming new infrastructure. Inner cities can experience a flood of new jobs and investment. And rising crime can give way to safe and prosperous communities.

All of these things, and so much more, are possible. But to accomplish them, we must replace the present policy of globalism – which has moved so many jobs and so much wealth out of our country – and replace it with a new policy of Americanism.

Under this American System, every policy decision we make must pass a simple test: does it create more jobs and better wages for Americans? If we lower our taxes, remove destructive regulations, unleash the vast treasure of American energy, and negotiate trade deals that put America First, then there is no limit to the number of jobs we can create and the amount of prosperity we can unleash. [1]

ANALYZING TRUMP'S SPEECH ON CREATING JOBS

My plan will embrace the truth that people flourish under a minimum government burden, and it will tap into the incredible unrealized potential of our workers and their dreams.

Donald Trump understands that less government and less burdensome regulations on the Private sector helps to release the forces of the free market instead of constricting them. In such an environment business thrives and the force of American entrepreneurship is unleashed to create more jobs. Small businesses are the fuel behind employment in America, but these small businesses have been crushed by burdensome government regulations of the last eight years.

> *Right now, 92 million Americans are on the sidelines, outside the workforce, and not part of our economy. It's a silent nation of jobless Americans.*

The above statement underscores why everyday Americans and Blue-collar democrats in the blue states of Wisconsin, Michigan and Pennsylvania crossed the aisle to vote for a loud-spoken political outsider, like Donald Trump. They knew that he knew what they were going through. He gave a voice to the over 92 million Americans who were left on the sidelines of unemployment and then forgotten. He called them the "silent nation of jobless Americans."

> *Look no further than the city of Flint, where I just visited. The jobs have stripped from this community, and its infrastructure has collapsed. In 1970, there were more than 80,000 people in Flint working for* GM *– today it is less than 8,000. Now Ford has announced it is moving all small car production to Mexico.*

What has happened to the city of Flint, in Michigan is truly a sad story of American decline. When I first went to Michigan in 1998 to minister for the church of a friend of mine, what I found then was a flourishing city. Today the city of Flint is an American nightmare. The jobs have left and the infrastructure of the city has collapsed. In his speech candidate Donald Trump stated that there was 80,000 people in Flint-Michigan who were working for GM in 1970 and that currently there was only 8000 people in Flint who were working for GM. By mentioning these figures he was letting it sink in that the city of Flint was a microcosm of what was happening in the heartland of America; Jobs leaving by the thousands to other countries. Donald Trump's understanding of the unemployment situation in many American cities may be the reason he is so focused on creating jobs even as the President in waiting.

> *My economic plan rejects the cynicism that says our labor force will keep declining, that our jobs will keep leaving, and that our economy can never grow as it did once before. We reject the pessimism that says our standard of living can no longer rise, and that all that's left to do is divide up and redistribute our shrinking resources. Everything that is broken today can be fixed, and every failure can be turned into a great success.*

This aspect of the Trump speech on "Jobs and the economy" is rooted in his "Think Big and Kick Ass" mindset that has driven him for most of his life in business. As someone who has read his New York Times best selling book *Think Big and Kick Ass*, I know the mindset that grafted that statement in his speech. Donald J Trump refuses to live in a world where accepting less becomes a way of life in America. Unfortunately most of our Beltway politicians have already bent over and backwards to accommodate globalists who are determined to ship jobs of Americans to other countries in the name of free trade. Even President

Obama and Hillary Clinton on separate occasions during the campaign trail told the American people to get used to the fact that some jobs are never coming back to America. Trump on the other hand categorically rejects this type of thinking. I believe this is the reason he is going to be one of the greatest jobs President the United States has ever produced.

> *Jobs can stop leaving our country, and start pouring in. Failing schools can become flourishing schools. Crumbling roads and bridges can become gleaming new infrastructure. Inner cities can experience a flood of new jobs and investment. And rising crime can give way to safe and prosperous communities.*

This aspect of the Trump speech shows us how Trump's contagious enthusiasm and positive attitude about America can lead to a new American century of prosperity. I am a firm believer that everything rises and falls on leadership. When a country has a leader who is very optimistic about the chances of jobs returning to America, it wont be long before we begin to see job creation in America on a massive scale. This aspect of the Trump speech also shows us how he intends to create jobs. He will start the engine of job creation by fixing our crumbling roads and bridges.

Many of these construction jobs are going to benefit African Americans and other minorities who are living in America's inner cities. Nowhere is there more need for new infrastructure than in the inner cities where most roads and buildings are completely dilapidated.

President-elect Trump is already proposing a $1 trillion investment into the rebuilding of crumbling roads and bridges in America's heartland.

> *All of these things, and so much more, are possible. But to accomplish them, we must replace the present policy of globalism – which has moved so many jobs and so much wealth out of our country – and replace it with a new policy of Americanism.*

In Trumpian tell-it-like-it-is style he believes the cancer that has been metastasizing on the American economy and destroying our resources is globalism. Globalist policies on both sides of the political divide in the name of free trade has been the number one culprit behind the bleeding of American jobs to foreign nationals. Consequently after over four decades of globalism, rising unemployment and the absence of manufacturing plants in Michigan and Pennsylvania just to name a few, inform us of the dangers of unchecked globalism. This is why Trump's America first policy is very important to understanding his philosophy behind creating an avalanche of new American jobs.

> *Under this American System, every policy decision we make must pass a simple test: does it create more jobs and better wages for Americans? If we lower our taxes, remove destructive regulations, unleash the vast treasure of American energy, and negotiate trade deals that put America First, then there is no limit to the number of jobs we can create and the amount of prosperity we can unleash.*

This aspect of Trump's speech on "Jobs and the economy" gets us into the heart of his "America First" policy. "*Under this American System, every policy decision we make must pass a simple test: does it create more jobs and better wages for Americans.*" How can a President who thinks this way and uses such a litmus test, fail to become a job creating machine? How many politicians in both parties who are bought and paid for by lobbyists, possess this America first mindset? If they were, they wouldn't have passed so many job killing trade deals with China, Mexico and India just to name a few. The United States of America has a trade deficit with all of these countries, which means money and jobs are leaving the USA on a one-way street.

TRUMP ALREADY SAVING JOBS!!!

It did not take President-elect Trump a longtime to begin to save American jobs. He did not wait to be officially inaugurated as the 45th President of the United States before he began to work for the American people. While the biased Liberal news media are refusing to give him his props, the American people are invigorated to have a President who is so focused on returning jobs back to the United States of America. On November 24, on the eve of Thanksgiving, President-elect sent out the following tweet.

> *I am working hard, even on Thanksgiving, trying to get Carrier A.C. Company to stay in the U.S. (Indiana). MAKING PROGRESS - Will know soon!* [2]

On November 29, 2016, Breitbart News released the following report about the deal President-elect Trump and Governor Mike Pence reached with the parent company of Carrier to save 1000 jobs that were scheduled to move to Mexico. As a matter of fact, candidate Trump brought the issue of Carrier moving its plant to Mexico and firing its employees to the national forefront. He talked about it often in his campaign rallies. As soon as he became President-elect he made a phone call to the CEO of the parent company of Carrier to work out a deal to stop the loss of jobs to Mexico. In Trumpian fashion, he made the deal and announced it on Twitter. Immediately after this deal was done, I remember watching an employee of Carrier on CNN who said, he had not voted for Trump but was very delighted that the President-elect had gone out of his way to save his job.

Small businesses are the fuel behind employment in America, but these small businesses have been crushed by burdensome government regulations.

"President-elect Donald Trump and Carrier have reached a deal that will keep nearly 1,000 factory jobs in Indiana, the company said on Tuesday," Indianapolis Fox 59 local news station reported.

> *Carrier Corporation announced the deal on Twitter.*
>
> *"We are pleased to have reached a deal with President-elect Trump & VP-elect Pence to keep close to 1,000 jobs in Indy. More details soon," Carrier Corporation's Twitter account reported on Tuesday evening.* [3]

Days after, at his transition headquarters at Trump Tower, the President-elect came down the elevator standing next to a Japanese investor who decided to invest $50 billion-dollars into the United States after a meeting with Trump. The investment will create an additional 50,000 jobs. President-elect Donald Trump also announced the addition of roughly 8,000 new jobs for Americans. 5,000 of that number are due to jobs that telecommunications giant Sprint will bring back from around the world. Trump also said the other 3,000 jobs will be hires from a new company called One Web. The President-elect spoke to members of the news media from his Mar a Largo estate in Palm Beach, Florida. "They're coming back to the United States, which is a nice change," he declared.

17

RESTORE LAW & ORDER

RECENT EVENTS, such as the killing of five police officers in Dallas, the terrorist attacks on a gay nightclub in Orlando, the toxic racial tone that Black Lives Matter is inciting in all Americans, plus the unprecedented murders of innocent people in Chicago (mostly black on black homicides) has compelled me to write my thoughts as to why I, an African American, voted for Donald J. Trump in November 2016. I especially implore my fellow African Americans (whose vote has been taken for granted by the Democratic Party for many years) to pay special attention to what I am about to say.

DONALD TRUMP IS NOT A RACIST!

I must admit that talking to my fellow African Americans about the possibilities of a Trump presidency, when they were so emotionally invested in Hillary Clinton, was quite difficult to say the least. This is because many of them had already been convinced by the biased mainstream media that Donald Trump was a racist. Once you have been labeled as a racist it's very difficult to shed the title. This is because accusing someone of being a racist is designed to make people shift from thinking with their minds to thinking with their emotion. Whether we admit it or not we all have inherent racial pride and prejudices. This is true of all races, including African-Americans. For me, believing the lie that Trump was a racist was a pill I could not swallow. The reason was very simple. I started following Donald Trump years before he ever thought of running for office. I followed him on TV and read his books, like *Think Big & Kick Ass* and *The Art of the Deal*!

What is quite interesting to me is that even though Donald Trump has lived in the public eye for so many years no one from either side of the political divide ever called him a racist. Thank God for YouTube, because we can use this social media platform to go back in time and watch videos about Donald Trump before he ran for office. As far back as the1980's when Oprah Winfrey was interviewing him, he was saying the same things that he was saying on the campaign trail. He believed then that China was eating our lunch on trade.

Oprah Winfrey jokingly asked him whether he would run for office someday. Do yourself a favor, go on YouTube and search for this particular video and you will be refreshingly surprised. Donald Trump told Oprah Winfrey that he would only run for office if he really thought things in the country where going from bad to worse. No one in the news media or in Washington, D.C. accused him of being a racist.

Many members of the media elite who were attacking him ferociously during his historic campaign and saying he was a racist were the same people, who couldn't wait to dine with the "Donald" at Trump Tower or many of his luxurious country clubs. Where was their outrage then? When Rev. Jesse Jackson was running for the presidency of the United States in 1988 Donald Trump was one of the businessmen who supported his presidential campaign. Even though Rev. Jesse Jackson was running on the Democratic ticket there was no outrage from either the news media or Democrats that he was allowing a man who was a racist to support his presidential campaign. Why the deafening silence? Why was there no outrage from the African-American community then? The answer, everybody then new that Donald Trump was not a racist.

So how does one suddenly become a racist after more than four decades of living in the public eye? It's called dirty politics my friend. For liberals and Democrats who love playing the card of "identity politics" every election cycle, calling Trump a racist was not even an original trick. It was same the playbook, but why change it, if African Americans and other minorities buy it so easily?

Why am I spending so much time on a chapter on law and order trying to explain that Donald Trump is not a racist? I'm doing it for the benefit of my fellow African Americans and other minorities who bought into the lie that he is a racist. It will be difficult for minorities and people of color to appreciate the much-needed law and order policies that President-elect Donald Trump proposed in Wisconsin if he is seen as a racist by people living in communities that desperately need effective policing? This distorted view of our president will make it difficult for him to make inner cities safe for African Americans and other minorities who live in these neighborhoods.

IT'S TIME FOR LAW & ORDER

Unless you are living on another planet or country, you know about the rising crime wave in America, especially in its inner cities. In Chicago, President Obama's hometown, they have been over 4000 homicides since 2009. This is both outrageous and unacceptable. One would think you're talking about Afghanistan or some town in Iraq, not in a modern American city. I know some African-American pastors who pastor in the inner city but can't wait to get back to the safety of the suburbs where they live. They too are terrified of the crime wave in the Democrat controlled city of Chicago.

According to the website baltimorecountymd.gov, crime statistics in 2015 for the City of Baltimore will put the fear of God in your heart. In 2015 homicides were up 25% from the previous year. Forcible rape crimes in 2015 were up 171.7%! Can you wrap your minds around this number? Attempted rape crimes in 2015 were up 64.3% in the same year. Most of the victims of these horrible crimes were African Americans and other minorities who live in the inner cities of Baltimore. It doesn't take a rocket scientist to figure out that these communities don't need less policing; they need more of a police presence in the neighborhood to deter crime.

What about the crime wave caused by illegal immigrants? This too has become a blight on American society. The problem of a porous border and not having a proper vetting system for people coming to the country is that you end up admitting people into the country who are career criminals in their countries of origin. Donald Trump was right to raise the issue of illegal immigration and point out that some of the people coming through our southern border with Mexico are perennial drug dealers, murderers and rapists. While it's also true that many of the illegal immigrants are decent and peace loving people, law and order must be enforced before the United States disintegrates into a Third World nation.

The murder of Kate Steinle by a homeless man, Juan Francisco Lopez-Sanchez, took the country by storm and highlighted the growing problem of crimes committed by illegal immigrants. Bill O'Reilly campaigned for and made an impassioned plea to members of Congress to pass "Kate's Law" to protect American citizens from crimes such as this that could be clearly anticipated and avoided. Lopez-Sanchez is an illegal immigrant from Mexico who had previously been deported on five different occasions. The shooting sparked controversy over San Francisco's status as a sanctuary city. President-elect Donald Trump cited this case in support of his proposal to deport foreign nationals living illegally in the United States. Donald Trump also mentioned Kate Steinle's murder during his acceptance speech at the Republican national convention in Cleveland.

TRUMP'S LAW & ORDER SPEECH!

When there were riots in Milwaukee, Wisconsin, President-elect Donald Trump made a campaign stop in Milwaukee. At this campaign stop the "Donald" made an impassioned plea for law and order in the United States. In his speech, he made it very clear that the police are not the problem behind the lack of law and order in the United States of America, particularly in the inner cities. Below is an excerpt of that famous speech.

"It's so great to be here tonight. I am honored to also be joined this evening by Governor Scott Walker, Chairman Reince Priebus, and Mayor Rudy Giuliani.

We are at a decisive moment in this election.

Last week, I laid out my plan to bring jobs back to our country. Yesterday, I laid out my plan to defeat Radical Islamic Terrorism. Tonight, I am going to talk about how to make our communities safe again from crime and lawlessness.

Let me begin by thanking the law enforcement officers here in this city, and across this country, for their service and sacrifice in difficult times. The violence, riots and destruction that have taken place in Milwaukee is an assault on the right of all citizens to live in security and peace. Law and order must be restored. It must be restored for the sake of all, but most especially the sake of those living in the affected communities.

The main victims of these riots are law-abiding African-American citizens living in these neighborhoods. It is their jobs, their homes, their schools and communities which will suffer as a result.

There is no compassion in tolerating lawless conduct. Crime and violence is an attack on the poor, and will never be accepted in a Trump administration.

The narrative that has been pushed aggressively for years now by our current Administration, and pushed by my opponent Hillary Clinton, is a false one. The problem in our poorest communities is not that there are too many police, the problem is that there are not enough police. More law enforcement, more community engagement, more effective policing is what our country needs.

Just like Hillary Clinton is against the miners, she is against the police. You know it, and I know it.

Those peddling the narrative of cops as a racist force in our society – a narrative supported with a nod by my opponent – share directly in the responsibility for the unrest in Milwaukee, and many other places within our country.

They have fostered the dangerous anti-police atmosphere in America. Everytime we rush to judgment with false facts and narratives – whether in Ferguson or in Baltimore – and foment further unrest, we do a direct disservice to poor African-American residents who are hurt by the high crime in their communities.

During the last 72 hours, while protestors have raged against the police here in Milwaukee, another 9 were killed in Chicago and another 46 were wounded. More than 2,600 people have been shot in Chicago since the beginning of the year, and almost 4,000 killed in President Obama's hometown area since his presidency began.

> *How are we serving these American victims by attacking law enforcement officers? The war on our police must end. It must end now. The war on our police is a war on all peaceful citizens who want to be able to work and live and send their kids to school in safety. Our job is not to make life more comfortable for the rioter, the looter, the violent disruptor. Our job is to make life more comfortable*

> *for the African-American parent who wants their kids to be able to safely walk the streets. Or the senior citizen waiting for a bus. Or the young child walking home from school. For every one violent protestor, there are a hundred moms and dads and kids on that same city block who just want to be able to sleep safely at night. My opponent would rather protect the offender than the victim.* [1]

BLUE LIVES MATTER!

How are we serving these American victims by attacking law enforcement officers? The war on our police must end. It must end now. The war on our police is a war on all peaceful citizens who want to be able to work and live and send their kids to school in safety. Our job is not to make life more comfortable for the rioter, the looter, the violent disruptor. Our job is to make life more comfortable for the African-American parent who wants their kids to be able to safely walk the streets. Or the senior citizen waiting for a bus. Or the young child walking home from school. For every one violent protestor, there are a hundred moms and dads and kids on that same city block who just want to be able to sleep safely at night. My opponent would rather protect the offender than the victim." [2]

The above excerpt of the Trump speech on "Law & Order" demands further introspection if you are going to understand Trump's appreciation for members of law enforcement. He poses the question, "*How are we serving these American victims by attacking law enforcement officers?*" The answer is self-evident.

Each time we attack law-enforcement officers and single them out as the problem in our communities we do a great disservice to the victims of crime in our communities.

When it matters most, when a house burglary or a rape is in progress, it's not members of the mainstream media that you want to see coming through your front door. It is the men in blue that you want to see come through the front door. Why? They represent the force for good in our society. But in our politically toxic culture of political correctness it is difficult to appreciate some of the tactics that members of law enforcement sometimes have to employ in order to deter crime. Mayor Rudi Giuliani saw a rapid decrease in crime in New York City because of the tactic called "stop and frisk." Many of the lives this tactic saved were African Americans and other minorities. But in today's culture of political correctness this battle-tested measure for effective policing cannot be applied in most high crime Cities that desperately need it.

The war on our police is a war on all peaceful citizens who want to be able to work and live and send their kids to school in safety. Our job is not to make life more comfortable for the rioter, the looter, the violent disruptor. Our job is to make life more comfortable for the African-American parent who wants their kids to be able to safely walk the streets.[3]

In 2016 being a police officer in the United States of America became a very dangerous assignment indeed: which is really sad to say. Some members of law enforcement were killed while having coffee in their patrol car. The rise of Black Lives Matter (BLM) and the biased mainstream news media concocted a very toxic environment against members of law enforcement. It was not a surprise when deranged far-left vigilantes began to target the police for assassination. This media hyped war on our police culminated in the shooting of five police officers in the city of Dallas, Texas. While the mainstream media was pushing this fake war-on-black-people by the police narrative, crime begun to go up in the inner cities as members of law enforcement became more timid in their policing. Who can blame them?

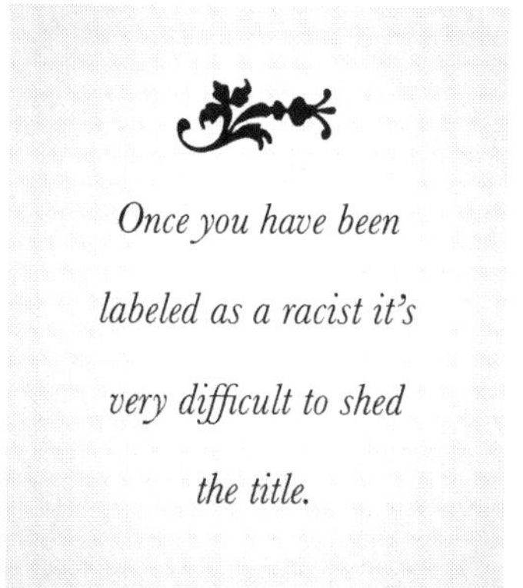

While it is very true that black lives matter, it's equally true that blue lives matter as well. I am not naïve; I know that there are some bad apples even among members of law enforcement. Candidate Trump made it very clear that these bad apples in law enforcement will be dealt with severely and in the appropriate manner. But he also made it very clear that the police are not the problem behind the collapse of law and order. Many of these men and women in blue place their lives on the line each time they put on the blue uniform. They deserve our respect and not our contempt. Most importantly they deserve due process when things go sour and not be judged guilty in the court of public opinion before they get their fair shake in court.

WHAT ABOUT BLACK LIVES MATTER?

As an African American I am very compassionate towards the cause of BLM. I'm sympathetic but deeply disagree with how this movement and its leaders have gone about making its case to the American public. From a branding perspective, the label *Black Lives Matter* is actually self-defeating because it negates the importance of other lives that are not black. In my humble opinion a better name for the movement should've been black lives matter also! A political movement such as the latter I could get behind. But it became clear to me that "Black Lives Matter" did not represent me after I watched Gov. O'Malley get slaughtered politically by the mainstream media and the leaders of the BLM movement when he said "all lives matter!" You would've thought that he insulted Jesus Christ in the middle of a church service from the way they reacted against him .Christian or not the expression "all lives matter" is a very reasonable position. The political backlash was so heavy; poor Gov. O'Malley had to walk back his very reasonable statement in order to once again become politically correct. So sad!

As an African-American who appreciates how far the United States has come, in the area of race relations, I further distanced myself from Black Lives Matter when I watched on television BLM demonstrators walking through the streets of Manhattan. When they were chanting, "pigs in a blanket fry 'em like bacon." Soon after this deplorable demonstration against members of law enforcement, cops begun to get shot by vigilantes who had received their marching orders.

I must confess; I have been a victim of racism in both South Africa and the United States of America. Much of that was from ordinary citizens, but once I experienced real racism from a white cop who stopped me by the side of the road in Texas. But this is the only time I have ever had a bad experience with law enforcement. For the most part my encounters with members of law enforcement when I was caught speeding have been very professional. My point is that it is very dangerous to paint all members of law enforcement with one brush stroke.

All men and women in uniform, whether police officers, firemen, or service personnel, deserve our utmost respect and consideration for without their sacrifice our lives would indeed be lived in chaos and fear. Hold them accountable, absolutely. This is the basis of our bill of rights. Malign them: absolutely not!

18

STAND WITH ISRAEL!

"I will bless those who bless you, and I will curse him who curses you; and in you all the families of the earth shall be blessed." Genesis 12:3

AS A PERSON OF FAITH nothing is more important to me on Trump's agenda than his fervent pledge to stand with Israel. If President Trump stands by his pledge to stand with Israel, God will shower our country will divine providence that will help "Make America Great Again!" Israel is our best and only ally in the Middle East. Every American president, both Republican and Democrat has, for the most part, demonstrated the United States' longstanding pledge to stand with Israel, until the Obama administration. I cannot remember an American administration that has been more openly hostile to Israel than the Obama administration. It's obvious that there has been no love lost between President Obama and Prime Minister Netanyahu. President Obama has shown more passion to work with Muslim nations, including those that are State sponsors of terrorism like Iran and the Palestinians. I have heard one commentator say that six words sum up this administration: *please Muslims, hate Christians, blame Israel.*

How else do you explain the Obama administration giving the Iranians $150 billion dollars in the so-called Iranian nuclear deal while knowing full well that Iran is the main financing mechanism behind terrorist organizations like Hezbollah and Hamas, to name a few. In the eight years that President Obama has been in office, I have never seen either him or Secretary Kerry, make such a scathing 70-minute speech against the Iranians or Palestinians with the same passion Secretary Kelly used to censure our number one ally in the Middle East.

I am really afraid for the United States' future when our government takes such a hostile tone towards Israel. Biblical history has shown that nations have risen and fallen over how they treat the nation of Israel. Ancient Egypt was the superpower of the ancient world, until the God of Israel brought it to its knees because of the enslavement and mistreatment of its Jewish population. Israel is the only nation on record that has the God of the Bible as its founder, with the United States of America is a distant second. Israel's miraculous survival and victory in the war of 1967 when it was still a young fledging nation underscores its partnership with the Divine.

"Then you shall say to Pharaoh, 'Thus says the LORD, "Israel is My son, My firstborn. 23"So I said to you, 'Let My son go that he may serve Me'; but you have refused to let him go. Behold, I will kill your son, your firstborn." Exodus 4:22-23

THE DISASTROUS U.N. SECURITY COUNCIL RESOLUTION

In a news article by Sean Savage for Jerusalem News Service, he makes a very intelligent analysis about the disastrous U.N. Security Council resolution against Israel, which the Obama administration actually championed in backroom deals with the four non-permanent members of the Security Council who brought this resolution before the Council.

"With the U.S. abstaining from Friday's vote, rather than exercising its veto power, the United Nations Security Council adopted a resolution condemning Israeli settlement construction beyond the 1967 lines.

The resolution was put forward Friday by four non-permanent Security Council members—New Zealand, Malaysia, Venezuela and Senegal—just a day after Egypt, which had originally sponsored the resolution, withdrew under pressure from President-elect Donald Trump and Israel. Both Trump and Israel called on the Obama administration to veto the resolution.

The resolution demands that Israel "immediately and completely cease all settlement activities in the 'occupied' Palestinian territory, including east Jerusalem," while also saying that the establishment of Israeli settlements has "no legal validity and constitutes a flagrant violation under international law."

> *While the resolution's passage is likely to do little to sway Israeli policies, the decision not to veto by outgoing President Barack Obama, who has had a tenuous and sometimes hostile relationship with Israeli Prime Minister Benjamin Netanyahu during the last eight years, marks a substantial break from the longstanding American policy of defending Israel against one-sided resolutions criticizing the Jewish state in the world body."* [1]

This disastrous U.N. Security Council resolution calls for the nation of Israel to actually retreat back to the indefensible borders it had back in 1967! The Obama administration in cohorts with nations on the Security Council that are hostile to Israel actually want Israel to unilaterally relinquish both its historical and biblical right to East Jerusalem and the Western Wall, which is also the location of its holiest site, the Temple Mount. Have you been to Israel lately? The Western Wall and East Jerusalem are as much part of Israel as Manhattan and Long Island are an integral part of New York. All this disastrous U.N. Security Council resolution does is make it easy for Palestinians to take legal action against Israel at the International Criminal Court in Hague. The one-sided resolution also gives the Palestinian Authority, the moral authority to accuse Israel of being in violation of this United Nations Security Council resolution. How ironic, when you consider the fact that the Palestinian Authority is actually on record for paying monthly salaries to terrorists, who kill Israelis.

ALAN DERSHOWITZ GOES OFF ON OBAMA:

When you are Obama and you start shedding the support of Democratic liberals, like Chuck Schumer and Alan Dershowitz, you know that you have made a major gaff. According to the conservative news site, The-Gateway-Pundit, Alan Dershowitz, a longtime Obama supporter, was furious with the Obama administration for what it did to Israel in refusing to veto the one-sided United Nations Security Council resolution. Alan Dershowitz, the longtime liberal attorney in the U.S. went off on President Obama.

He stated on "FOX and Friends" that Obama may be "the worst foreign policy President ever." The fact of the matter is that the Obama administration's refusal to stand with Israel in this case has garnered bipartisan criticism. The only good news for Israel is that it doesn't have long to wait to welcome a new American administration that is staunchly pro-Israel. The Trump administration can do a lot to blunt the consequences of this United Nations Security Council resolution against Israel.

HOPEFUL TWEETS

Supporters and foes who followed the amazing and unusual campaign of President-elect Trump knows that we have never seen a political candidate in U.S. history who has tweeted himself into the White House like the "Donald!" He has discovered that his twitter account is more powerful in getting out his message to the American public than the biased mainstream media. In Trumpian fashion, when the United States abstained on a crucial U.N. Security Council resolution condemning Israel for its settlements on the Western Wall and East Jerusalem, Trump sent out a tweet in defense of Israel.

> *The big loss yesterday for Israel in the United Nations will make it much harder to negotiate peace. Too bad, but we will get it done anyway!* [2]

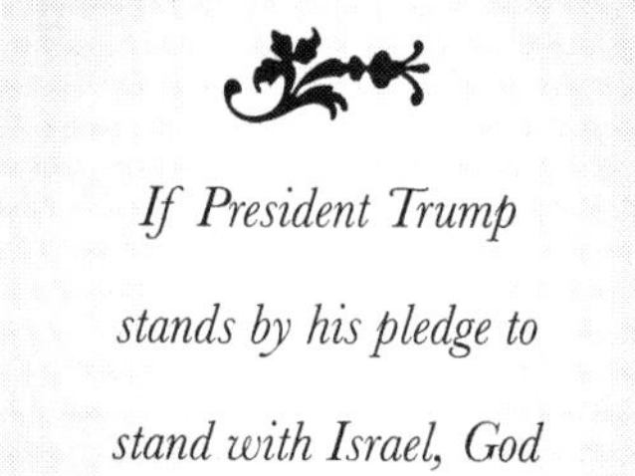

On December 28, 2016 Secretary John Kerry gave a very lamentable speech trying to explain why the Obama administration abstained on the crucial United Nation Security Council resolution condemning Israel for its settlements on the Western Wall and East Jerusalem. In the speech that betrayed the Obama administration's hostility towards the nation of Israel, Secretary John Kerry spent more time censuring and lecturing the nation of Israel than he did the Palestinians. You would of have thought by listening to his speech that the number one culprit for the lack of peace in the Middle East is the State of Israel. Never mind that the Palestinian Authority of President Mahmoud Abbas does little to discourage its citizen's militant aggression against innocent Israeli citizens. Prime Minister Benjamin Netanyahu's calls for peace talks with President Mahmoud Abbas have gone an unanswered for quite a while.

Speaking on Fox News "Your World with Neil Cavuto," Mayor of Israel Nir Barrat made an interesting argument concerning the challenges to the two State solution and peace negotiations between Israel and the Palestinians. "Israel recognizes the validity of a Palestinian state but up to now the Palestinians do not recognize the right of Israel to exist as a state. How can you have peace negotiations with people who don't even recognize your rights to exist as a State?" He declared.

Personally, I was most astounded by the part of Sec. John Kerry's speech, in which he said, "Israel can either be Jewish or democratic, it cannot be both!" How insane and condescending is this? Do you mean to tell me that Israel cannot be both Jewish and democratic at the same time? Its no wonder the Obama foreign policy in the Middle East has been a train wreck. Libya, Iraq, are up in flames, Syria an Isis haven and thousands of Syrians dead in a brutal civil war, tell us all we need to know about the failure of the Obama-Clinton-Kerry foreign policy. Immediately after Secretary Kerry's speech defending the U.S.'s decision to abstain in the U.N. vote, President-elect Trump sent out another hopeful tweet about the future of U.S.-Israel relationship.

> *We cannot continue to let Israel be treated with such disdain and disrespect. They used to have a great friendship in the U.S, but not anymore. The beginning of the end was the horrible Iran deal, and now this (U.N.)! Stay strong Israel, January 20th is fast approaching!* [3]

Immediately after President-elect's tweet, Prime Minister Benjamin Netanyahu responded to Trump's tweet.

President-elect Trump, thank you for your warm friendship and your clear-cut support for Israel! [4]

TRUMP: AMERICA'S MOST PRO-ISRAEL PRESIDENT

When candidate Trump was running for the presidency during the Republican primaries, he gave a rousing speech at the AIPAC conference in support of an ongoing favorable American policy toward our number one democratic ally in the Middle East, Israel. In what is my favorite Trump speech, the "Donald" minced no words establishing his historical support for Israel. He continued pronouncing his support for Israel in each Trump rally that followed thereafter, up to the day of the election. Below is a short transcript of Trump's AIPAC speech.

TRUMP: *Good evening. Thank you very much. I speak to you today as a lifelong supporter and true friend of Israel. I am a newcomer to politics, but not to backing the Jewish state. In 2001, weeks after the attacks on New York City and on Washington and, frankly, the attacks on all of us, attacks that perpetrated and they were perpetrated by the Islamic fundamentalists, Mayor Rudy Giuliani visited Israel to show solidarity with terror victims.*

I sent my plane because I backed the mission for Israel 100 percent. In spring of 2004 at the height of the violence in the Gaza Strip, I was the grand marshal of the 40th Salute to Israel Parade, the largest-single gathering in support of the Jewish state.

It was a very dangerous time for Israel and frankly for anyone supporting Israel. Many people turned down this honor. I did not. I took the risk and I'm glad I did. But I didn't come here tonight to pander to you about Israel. That's what politicians do: all talk, no action. Believe me.

I came here to speak to you about where I stand on the future of American relations with our strategic ally, our unbreakable friendship and our cultural brother, the only democracy in the Middle East, the state of Israel. Thank you.

My number-one priority is to dismantle the disastrous deal with Iran. Thank you. Thank you. I have been in business a long time. I know deal making. And let me tell you, this deal is catastrophic for America, for Israel and for the whole of the Middle East. [5]

DEFUND THE UN!

Both Republicans and Democrats in past U.S. administrations have toyed with the idea of the United States defunding the U.N. for its ongoing hostility towards Israel and the United States. But none have had the courage or political will to defund the U.N. Maybe in the political maverick, Donald Trump, America may finally have a president who possess both the courage and political will to send a very strong message to the United Nations, that the United States will no longer tolerate this demented campaign by the U.N. to delegitimize the only true democracy in the Middle East. The United Nations can no longer be a platform for rogue dictators to attack and mock the United States and Israel. The United States underwrites a quarter of the United Nations annual budget. Defunding, it even for one year, would send a very strong signal that the United States means business.

In an article written by Pam Key for Breitbart News on the 28th of December, 2016, law professor Alan Dershowitz had more things to say about what he thinks of the disastrous United Nations Security Council resolution condemning Israel. He also noted the unmistakable hostility that the United Nations, as a body, has against the nation of Israel by the overwhelming number of anti-Israel resolutions that the UN has undertaken compared to resolutions against the rest of the world.

"Wednesday on AM 970's "The Joe Piscopo Show," while discussing the recent United Nations security resolution criticizing Israel settlements, lawyer, author and emeritus law professor at Harvard University Alan Dershowitz said the United States needs to "threaten to defund the United Nations." Dershowitz said, "There is an automatic anti Israel bias at the UN. Consider the following story — this happened less than a year ago — the head of the UN Ban Ki-moon put Saudi Arabia on a blacklist of countries that mistreat children during wartime and the head of the Saudis called Ban Ki-moon and said unless you take us off of the blacklist we will stop sending money to the UN, and Ban Ki-moon said alright and he took them off the blacklist."

So money counts at the UN. And so what the United States should do now is threaten to defend the United Nations unless the Untied Nations stops showing this incredible bias against Israel," he continued. "Forty resolutions this year against Israel, four against the entire rest of the world at a time when Syria is imploding when Russia took over the Crimea. So many violations of human rights are occurring in the world. Forty resolution against Israel, only four against the rest of the world. That shows you something about the bias of that UN building." [6]

As a person of faith, biblical historian and as a patriotic American there is no more urgent oreign policy agenda than the U.S. reaffirming in word and deed our commitment to our number one ally in the entire Middle East- Israel. The Trump's administration must fightor a peace treaty between Israel and the Palestinians, which definitely involves a two-state solution without compromising Israel's historical and biblical right to claim Jerusalem as its official capital. President-elect Trump's hint to move the U.S. embassy from Tel Aviv to Jerusalem would be the most important gesture shown to Israel by a sitting American president since its restoration in 1948. *To falter in our support of Israel will curse us in the long run: we might go the way of ancient Egypt.*

Book: Source References

Endnotes: Chapter 1

1. 1.retrieved@: https://en.wikipedia.org/wiki/Donald_Trump_presidential_campaign,_2016

Endnotes: Chapter 2

1. retrieved @ www.donaldjtrump.com
2. retrieved @ https://represent.us/action/5-facts-lobbyists/
3. retrieved @ http://www.nationalreview.com/article/435864/clinton-cash-movie-proves-hillary-clinton-unfit-office

Endnotes: Chapter 3

1. Retrieved@ www.donaldjtrump.com
2. Retrieved@ www.donaldjtrump.com
3. Retrieved@ http://www.usnews.com/opinion/blogs/nancy-pfotenhauer/2012/07/03/four-flaws-of-obamacare
4. Retrieved@ http://reason.com/blog/2011/03/28/the-case-for-health-savings-ac
5. Retrieved@https://www.nga.org/files/live/sites/NGA/files/pdf/MAKINGMEDICAIDBETTER.pdf
6. Retrieved@ http://barrecavineyards.com/rules-for-radicals/

Endnotes: Chapter 4

1. Retrieved @ www.donaldjtrump.com

Endnotes: Chapter 5

1. Retrieved from: God's Chaos Candidate by Dr. Lance Walnau

Endnotes: Chapter 6

1. Retrieved: www.breitbart.com/.../merkel-new-year-speech-migrant-policy-terrorism- compassion/
2. Retrieved from: www.newsmax.com/politics/trump-republican...border/.../766189/
3. Retrieved from: www.donaldjtrump.com

Endnotes: Chapter 8

1. Retrieved from: www.breitbart.com/.../nick-cannon-planned-parenthood-founded- exterminate-negro-race/
2. Retrieved from: www.donaldjtrump.com

Endnotes: Chapter 10

1. Retrieved from: www.donaldjtrump.com

Endnotes: Chapter 11

1. Retrieved from: https://en.wikipedia.org/wiki/Inland_Regional_Center
2. Retrieved from: https://en.wikipedia.org/wiki/2016_Berlin_attack

3. Retrieved from: time.com/.../donald-trump-national-security-immigration-terrorism-speech

Endnotes: Chapter 12

1. http://www.wsj.com/articles/trump-picks-school-choice-advocate-betsy-devos-for-education-secretary-1479927146
2. Retrieved from: https://edexcellence.net/.../president-elect-donald-trump-quotes-about-education

Endnotes: Chapter 13

1. Retrieved from: www.donaldjtrump.com

Endnotes: Chapter 14

1. www.washingtontimes.com/.../1/monica-crowley-how-donald-trump-is-r...
2. Retrived from: www.donaldjtrump.com

Endnotes: Chapter 16

1. Retrieved from: time.com/4495507/donald-trump-economy-speech-transcript/
2. Retrieved from: twitter @realdonaldtrump
3. Retrieved from: www.breitbart.com/.../president-elect-donald-trump-cuts-deal-to-keep-

Endnotes: Chapter 17

1. Retrieved from: heavy.com/.../read-full-transcript-donald-trump-transcript-law-and-order...
2. Retrieved from: heavy.com/.../read-full-transcript-donald-trump-transcript-law-and-order...
3. Retrieved from: heavy.com/.../read-full-transcript-donald-trump-transcript-law-and-order...

Endnotes: Chapter 18

1. Retrieved from: http://www.jns.org/latest-articles/2016/12/23/in-major-us-shift-obama-admin-refuses-to-veto-un-measure-against-israeli-settlements#
2. Retrieved from: twitter @realdonaldtrump
3. Retrieved from: twitter @realdonaldtrump
4. Retrieved from: https://twitter.com/netanyahu
5. Retrieved from: time.com/4267058/donald-trump-aipac-speech-transcript/
6. Retrieved from: http://www.breitbart.com/video/2016/12/28/dershowitz-money-counts-un-u-s-needs-threaten-defund-un-anti-israel-bias/

Made in the USA
Lexington, KY
04 March 2017